MINISTERIAL ETHICS

Dr. Ronald L. Bernier

Copyright © 2011 – Dr. Ronald L. Bernier

Published by Vision Publishing
Ramona, California

ISBN 978-1-61529-024-6

FOR INFORMATION ON ORDERING PLEASE CONTACT:

Master Builder Ministries, INC.
397 Bay Street
Fall River, MA 02724
(508) 730-1735
www.mbministries.org

Or

Vision Publishing
1-800-9-VISION
www.visionpublishingservices.com

PRINTED IN THE UNITED STATES OF AMERICA

Contents

FORWARD

When I first learned that a very well-known minister of the Gospel had filed for divorce under a cloud of suspicion of financial and marital infidelity, I was in shock; my emotions turned to dismay, then anger, then sadness, and finally, reflection. You see, I knew (or thought I knew) this spiritual leader. His ministry was successful; lives in that community had been positively impacted over the years. Yet, here we were...scandal, shame, and serious questions. Was this dynamic leader really saved? Without question. Gifted? Absolutely. He had a meteoric rise though he had minimal formal theological education. This man was quick, entrepreneurial, and seemed to have a Midas touch on his life, with a devoted spouse and three well-mannered children. So, how could someone with so many wonderful things going for him choose to walk away from the church, family, community, and call?

Well, one can never fully know all of the dynamics of success or failure, rise or fall. One thing has to be considered, and that is, what foundation of character was formed under this sterling example of success and failure? Could it be that this dazzling rise to fame could not be sustained because of the lack of character? Without an integrated ethic built on the solid rock of Jesus Christ and His word, we are all similarly vulnerable.

Both the 20th and 21st centuries have seen a fairly radical shift in fundamental worldview. From modernist to post-modernist, from absolutes to relativism, much of our culture's ethics and convictions have become mere suggestions to consider, not absolutes to which one commits. This post-modern relativism has lead many to build their ethical lives on the shifting sands of public opinion. More messages are preached today from the commentary of Fox News and CNN, than from strong and diligent exegesis of the Word. These "modern" trends toward the shallow for relevance sake, the politicization of church life, and the acceptance of the pursuit of gold and glory as our spiritual right have not helped the church to sustain its rightful place as the standard bearer of salt and light for our world.   Most learned and sincere spiritual leaders (of which the vast majority of pastors are) are strongly resisting this trend, and this will always be, for nothing can stop the forward advance of Christ's glorious kingdom.

I have concluded that this excellently thought-out and well written work by my friend and co-laborer for Christ, Dr. Ron Bernier, is not for the fully committed religious superstar who has freely chosen relativistic compromise as his modus operandi. It is for the vast majority of spiritual leaders who are standing firm on "the faith once delivered for the saints"; a book strongly recommended as a resource to counterpunch our modern culture's worldview. This book is for the young man or woman, or those young in the faith, who love God with a sincere heart, desiring, above all, to serve Christ without compromise.   This book will aid its readers in establishing an ethical, biblical foundation for their lives which will sustain them throughout long, faithful, and successful (according to God's perspective) lives of service in the marketplace or in the church. For the student of the Word, for the young man or woman in discipleship under their pastor, for the minister of the Gospel who may not have had the privilege of having his character challenged by Christ and His Word…this book is a gift that will lead to a journey of transformation.

Stan E. DeKovan, PhD.

Founder and President

Vision International University

INTRODUCTION

Stories of fallen clergy are not hard to find. Many of these accounts focus on sexual misconduct, but other kinds of misconduct are well represented, including the misappropriation of funds and the misuse of power. That these stories come to our attention through the media and other channels so regularly that we are more saddened than shocked by them bears witness to the critical nature of this problem. Clergy misconduct is a crisis which demands immediate attention.

Facing this present reality should not make us long for an innocent past when *"these things just didn't happen."* The history of the church serves as a poignant reminder that "these things" have *always* happened. The task before us is both critical and urgent, but at the same time perennial. Christian ethics and authentic discipleship are the critical and urgent task for *all* Christians of *every* age.

Christians who embrace the "priesthood of all believers" are doubly reminded of this truth. Since we believe that all Christians are called to minister, we must also affirm that following Jesus does not mean one thing for vocational ministers and something less for laity. We should not expect one level of discipleship and ethical behavior for pastors and other professional ministers and another level for church members whose ministries are lived out in secular work places. The high calling which is ours in Christ Jesus is just that – *ours*, the responsibility and privilege of the whole Body of Christ to serve God and God's creation in Christian ministry.

It is nonetheless the case that the call to follow Jesus which we hold in common is lived out in particular vocations. Being a professional minister in a local church raises categories of ethical conduct which are specific to professional ministry.

One of the greatest problems today, especially between ministers and churches, is the lack of, or violation of, Christian ethics. Jesus said that the "children of this world are wiser than the children of light" (Luke 16:8). This should not be so. When it comes to the matter of ethics, the professional world often puts the Christian profession to shame for failure in this area. The accounting, legal, medical and business professions have a code of ethics.

To some, the very words "Code of Ethics" conjure up some concept of letterism, legalism, and bondage to a set of rules and regulations.

We can define what is meant by "code of ethics."

Oxford Dictionary:

> **code:** Systematic collection of statutes, a body of laws so arranged as to avoid inconsistency and overlapping; a set of rules on any subject; prevalent morality of a society or class.

> **ethics:** Relating to morals, treating of moral questions; the science of morals, treatise of this, moral principles, rules of conduct, the whole field of science; conforming to a recognized standard.

> **etiquette:** Conventional rules of personal behavior in polite society; ceremonial of court; unwritten code restricting professional men or women in what concerns interest of their peers or dignity of their profession, especially Medical, Legal Etiquette.

Therefore, societal ethics are based on the basic common principles of proper human relationships and etiquette expected in society. The code of ethics is generally based on certain character and behavioral qualifications that are expected of those in the professional world. Christian ethics are based on the basic principles of the Bible and the relationships and courtesies that should be in the life of a Christian and more especially a person in the profession of a minister. "Profession" means "vocation or calling."

Ethics has to do with the proper conduct of a minister in his various relationships with people. The Christian minister, of all people, should have Biblically based character qualifications, and his ethics should be Biblically based.

Although "code of ethics" and "etiquette" are words not used expressly in the Bible, nevertheless they are Bible truth! The Scriptures outlay God's "code of ethics" for ministers either in: specific commands, such as in the Ten Commandments (Exodus 20); the Sermon on the Mount (Matthew 5, 6, 7), or in principles (1 Corinthians 9:7-14). There are certain rules of conduct not specifically commanded in Scripture, but they arise out of Scriptural principles. Sometimes these principles have to be sought out and discovered and then applied to life's situations (Proverbs 25:2).

What follows is an attempt to name and describe some of the most important aspects of clergy ethics. First, we must define what a Christian view of ethics is, followed by establishing a foundation for clergy ethics by examining ministerial integrity, the stewardship of power and the biblical concept of covenant. Then we will explore why we must qualify leadership based on qualities spelled out in the New Testament.

In addition, we will look at a minister's call, relationships, stewardship of time, health, economic responsibilities, sexual conduct, and community involvement as we continue to explore specific aspects of ministerial ethics with an example of a Covenant of Ministerial Ethics that can be used by a minister and church to form some agreement as to mutual responsibilities.

In all of this we pray along with the Apostle Paul that *"we give no offense in anything, put no obstruction in anybody's way, so that no fault may be found and our ministry blamed or discredited"* (2 Corinthians 6:3 AMP).

CHAPTER 1
CHRISTIAN VIEW OF ETHICS

INTRODUCTION

"Ethics is in the first place a statement about God - who He is, how He acts, what He values. ... Ethical behavior is a consequence of man's becoming fully personal through the realization of his immediate relationship to the will and purpose of God."[i]

> Every person who engages in moral judgment implies by his judgment the existence of an objective moral order. This is because the relationship called judging involves at least three terms: the person who judges, the action that is judged, and the standard of judgment by which the judged action is measured. This last, if moral experience is to make sense at all, must be something independent of both of the other terms.[ii]"

Christian ethics goes back to God as the ultimate ground and source of morality."[iii] He is the supreme rule of right. He defines the whole content of morality by His own revealed will.

It is not merely because "in God is the perfect realization of the Ideal Righteousness," but because God legislates the nature of the good, that biblical ethics is a radical departure from the pagan view of the moral order.[iv]

Biblical ethics discredits an autonomous morality. ... The biblical view maintains always a dynamic statement of values, refusing to sever the elements of morality from the will of God.[v]

"The task of Christian ethics is determining what conforms to God's character and what does not."[vi] *"Thus, the beginning point of Christian ethics is not rules but the form of Christ and formation of*

the Church in conformity with the form of Christ." *vii*   *"The performance of God's will alone constitutes man's highest good."viii The Apostle Paul's perspective is the same.   The teaching of Romans 12:2 is that 'the good, the acceptable, the perfect is the will of God.'"ix The conflict between duty and happiness is resolved by the grace of God at work on the heart of the believer, "for it is God who works in you both to will and to do for His good pleasure" (Phil. 2:13 NKJ).*

The rule of life is to "seek first the Kingdom of God and His righteousness" (Mt. 6:33). The stress Jesus placed on the spiritual aspect of the Kingdom of God as the Rule of God in the lives of His servants reinforces this idea that the good life is submission to the sovereign God.x

MacLennan singles out as the most important conception in His teaching ... the living of life in wholehearted loyalty to God and unquestioning obedience to His will in this world here and now. He is urging upon men the seeing and accepting of the rule of God in their daily living. If they see and grasp that central reality of life, all else will fall into line and life will take on the power and a peace and joy which can be found no other way. ...It is clear that the Rule of God as taught by Jesus demands an obedience of a nature which is nothing less than a complete subordination of the human will to the will of God. The motto for any son of the Kingdom, as for Jesus Himself, is: "Not what I will but what You will." It is a demand quite as rigorous as ever made under the law.xi

The nature of man is to oppose law, thinking it limits his freedom. True liberty and conformity to law, however, are far from being mutually exclusive, they are in fact complementary:

> It is only when man walks along the path delineated by God's Commandments that he can realize true fulfillment of his personality. The law is not a tyrannical imposition, confining man and cramping his opportunity to enjoy life: on

14

the contrary, it is God's gracious revelation of the structure of the spiritual universe, which teaches man to move along the cosmos' lines of force rather than at cross-purpose with his true destiny.[xii]

"The will of God so reveals His character that the man who conforms to His commandments will exhibit the image of God in his life."[xiii]

The ultimate ethical purpose is the praise of God. God is praised as His will is done and obedience is the means to achieve this goal. Obedience is something we come into through a relational experience with God. This relationship is based upon a divine destiny for all of God's creation. There is a flow in which this relationship can be expressed: love that leads to fellowship that leads to service. We can further express the ethic of relationship by: the divine will, enablement, sanction, mission, and preparation.

DIVINE WILL - UNITY

God's divine will is to bring unity to all of life. Psalm 103:19 (NIV) says, *"The Lord has established His throne in heaven, and His kingdom rules over all."* The word *"establish"* means "to make secure or firm; to cause to be recognized and accepted; to set in a secure condition or position."[xiv] The word *"throne"* speaks of a sovereign rank or power, of the chair occupied by this sovereign one. His "kingdom" is the entire realm over which God's sovereignty extends, where He exercises limits and restraints as He governs. Without some form of government, lawlessness, anarchy and chaos result. In a larger perspective, Philippians 2:9-11 says *that the entire universe acknowledges that Jesus Christ is Lord to the glory of God the Father.* All existing things, including the earth and the heavens, will confess and admit to the reality and the truth that Jesus is Lord, bringing ultimate glory to God the Father. It also speaks of a time when the Church, God's instrument in the world, will come into full realization of it's ultimate destiny of growing in the image of God, functioning in interpersonal relationships and in fellowship, until the awaiting universe sees God in His Person revealed to redeemed men and women - forevermore.

Unity is attained and maintained by belief in one God (see Deut. 6:4). When we fail to maintain this relationship through disobedience, we come out of divine order only to be dominated by the one who has rebelled among the angels of God in Heaven and was cast down in judgment with punishment. Rebellion is an uprising or organized opposition intended to change or overthrow an existing government or ruling authority without the legal right or authority to do so. Rebellion is a problem in character which does not come under rule. The cross begins here with two opposing thoughts - self-will or God's will; rebellion or submission; self-authority or God's authority.

> The fallen world of ethical rebellion is depicted in Scripture as under the sway of Satan. It is a kingdom of darkness whose creatures are the servants of the evil one. Twice Jesus speaks of the unregenerate as "children of Satan" (Mt. 13:38; Jn. 8:44). He is the spirit that works in the "children of disobedience" (Eph. 2:2). The New Testament pinpoints the background for stark realities of evil in Satan himself." ..."Satan is described as the god of this world, blinding the minds of the unbelieving (2 Cor. 4:3). ...Satan remains as the defiant and influential power in the world of unbelief, which is in darkness (Col. 1:13). The cosmos uncommitted to the Christ is ruled by Satan (Eph.2:2; Mt.4:16; Lk. 22:53; Acts 26:18; Rom. 13:12; Eph. 5:8; 6:12). But all excuse for ignorance of the real Lord of heaven and earth is removed by Christ's resurrection (Acts 17:30).[xv]

Adam, God's first delegated human authority in the earth (see Gen. 1:28), was seduced along with Eve to come out from under the authority of God and thus came under divine judgment for his sin

16

(see Gen. 3:24). We, being sons in the flesh, have this sin imputed to us and are in need of a Savior to redeem us from our bondage. God continues to rule. When Jesus prayed in Matthew 6:10, "Thy Kingdom come," He was saying may we come under God's rule and order. The manifestation of God's Kingdom on earth will be fully realized when every hostile and wicked power is judged and salvation is attained by the righteous who have been redeemed from their burden of sin and receive the benefits of the Kingdom.

This kingship is not only as something in the future, but something present (see Lk. 17:21). It is God's rule, which we must receive as little children here and now (see Mk. 10:15), not only seeking the Kingdom for the future, but in our present existence (see Mt. 6:33; Lk. 12:31). The Kingdom has actually come among us in the person and works of Jesus (see Mt. 12:28). The message of the Kingdom is "God is near". He is confronting people with the challenge to decision. In the person of Christ, all that the prophets had hoped for and predicted has been realized. God has entered into history in His kingly power to defeat the powers of evil and to bring to people a foretaste of the blessings of the eschatological Kingdom while they still live in this present age. One of the most characteristic works of Jesus was freeing people from their demonic bondage. This is a sign of the presence of the Kingdom of God. This present defeat of Satan is also seen in the mission of Jesus' disciples (see Lk. 10:9, 17). This mighty working of the Kingdom of God requires a mighty response - "men of violence" must "take it by force". We must be willing and ready to engage in any action, however radical, in response to the presence of the Kingdom of God.

The book of Revelation pictures the plight of a persecuted Church in a hostile world, but assures the Church that Christ has already won a victory over the powers of evil (see Rev. 5:5) by virtue of which He can finally destroy them (see Rev. 19:11-20:14). Revelation closes with a highly symbolic picture of the Kingdom of

God (see chapters 21 and 22) when God comes to dwell among His people, and "They shall see His face..." (Rev. 22:4). Thus, the New Testament ends with "Divine order restored to a disordered world," unified through the belief in one God. This is the Kingdom of God.

Unity is also furthered through ethical obedience - not simply lip service, but an allegiance of the heart (see Amos 5:21-24; Is. 29:13; Deut. 6:5; Prov. 4:23), where motive becomes as important as action. The Sermon on the Mount in Matthew's gospel taught that heart issues were an important root to the tree and fruit of our lives. Jesus maintained that obedience or disobedience to the law began inwardly in the human heart. It is not sufficient to conform one's outward actions and words to that which the law required. The thought life must be conformed to the will of God as expressed in the law first of all (see Ps. 40:8; Heb. 10:7,9). When the mind is set to do the will of God, the speaking and acting will not deviate from it. Emphasis will be on the inward and spiritual aspects of religion rather than on the outward and material aspects.

> Matthew 5 describes God's radical reconstruction of the heart. Observe the sequence. First, *we recognize we are in need* (we're poor in spirit). Next, *we repent of our self-sufficiency* (we mourn). *We quit calling the shots and surrender control to God* (we're meek). *So grateful are we for His presence that we yearn for more of Him* (we hunger and thirst). *As we grow closer to Him, we become more like Him. We forgive others* (we're merciful). *We change our outlook* (we're pure in heart). *We love others* (we're peacemakers). *We endure injustice* (we're persecuted). *It's no casual shift in attitude. It is a demolition of the old structure and a creation of the new. The more radical the change, the greater the joy.*[xvi]

In accordance with God's will is His unchangeable character with certain moral attributes that belong to Him. These attributes are also those which God intends man to possess, and thus are called communicable attributes. God is holy (see Lev. 11-45) and, therefore, so should we be holy. God is also perfect (see Mt. 5:48), truth (see Heb. 6:18), love (see 1 John. 4:16), righteous (see Rom. 1:17), and faithful (see 1 Cor. 1:9). The moral character and qualities of God were manifested in Christ as the perfect man. These moral attributes are to be manifested in the believer also, as he is conformed to Christ. Only the Son of God, who was God incarnate, could give us a full and perfect revelation of the Father God. In Christ, God was clothed with the flesh of man. Jesus Christ was the fullest and clearest revelation of the Father and Son relationship that God desires the redeemed to come into by the new birth (see Jn. 1:14-18; 3:1-5; 14:9; 16:17; Mt. 5:45; 11:27; Ps. 103:13; 1 John. 3:1-2).

These distinctive characteristics set apart the redeemed community from the unregenerate. The redeemed are bound together by their belief in one God and share the purpose of being light and salt to the world. The destiny of each individual and the entire called out community is bound to a covenantal loyalty to one God, who both judges and blesses. God made man in His own image. His essential law for man is that he shall reflect the image of God and become like Him in character, demonstrating love that fulfills His covenants, faithfulness that discharges its responsibilities (see Lam. 3:23; Prov. 28:20), truthfulness that is reliable (see Ex. 34:6; Hos. 4:1), social concerns implemented in justice, with a balanced order that seeks compassionately to correct abuses (see Is. 30:18), righteousness that aims to conduct all its relationships with integrity and responsibility (Ps. 35:24; Deut. 6:25; Mk. 7:9).

DIVINE ENABLEMENT - FORGIVENESS

Every system of ethics must have some ultimate basis for goodness and obligation; God is the basis of Christian ethics. But why does God have authority over us? Why do we keep God's commandments? If we wish to respond by means of a coherent presentation of theology, there is more than one approach. One could start with human need. One could start by considering God's character, God's sovereignty, and God's intentions in creation and history and in the Law. But the question can be answered in terms of spiritual autobiography. The "why" now does not call for purely rational explanations, rather it asks why in fact you as a person seek to obey this God? It was with this question in mind that Karl Barth stated that God does not have authority over us because of a particular definition of God. We recognize this claim because God is "the God who is gracious to us in Christ Jesus." Barth here has encapsulated a central truth of New Testament theology and ethics. *Our obedience to God is inextricably bound up with our reception of divine grace in and following conversion.*[xvii]

> *...The law of the Spirit of life in Christ Jesus has made me free from the law of sin and death. For what the law could not do in that it was weak through the flesh, God did by sending His own Son in the likeness of sinful flesh, on account of sin: He condemned sin in the flesh,* (being sinless) *that the righteous requirement of the law might be fulfilled in us who do not walk according to the flesh but according to the Spirit* (Rom. 8:2-4).

With the Christian answer it is now possible to understand that there are true moral absolutes. There is no law behind God, because the farthest thing back is God. The moral absolutes rest upon God's character. The creation as He originally made it conformed to His character. The moral commands He has given to men are an expression of His character. Men as created in His image are to live by choice on the basis of what God is. The standards of morality are determined by what conforms to His character, while those things which do not conform are immoral. ...When man sins, he brings forth what is contrary to the moral law of the universe and as a result he is morally and legally guilty.

> Because man is guilty before the Lawgiver of the universe, doing what is contrary to His character, his sin is significant

20

in a significant history. Man has true moral guilt. This is entirely different from the conception of modern thought, which states that actions do not lead to guilt - a view within which actions thus become morally meaningless.[xviii]

To understand what the Apostle Paul means by the "law of sin and death," we must relate his understanding of both sin and flesh. In reading Romans 8, we have little difficulty grasping the significance of the flesh. The law is said to be "weak through the flesh" (v. 3). Those who live "according to the flesh" set their minds on the "things of the flesh", which we are told is death (vv. 5-6). The fleshly mind is "enmity against God" and is not subject to the law of God, nor can it be (v. 7). "Those who are in the flesh cannot please God" (v. 8). The flesh is an attitude or inclination operating in complete rejection of the divine will, which requires self-sacrificial submission, choosing instead the free expression of anything and everything that will bring self-gratification. So pervasive is the sinful propensity of the human nature, which seeks to be selfish and self-serving, that man recognizes he is incapable of breaking its power, resulting in being "sold under sin."

God's grace is found in His dealings with the sinful human nature. God gave the law, which could neither make man right with God, nor make him live rightly before God. God sent "His own Son in the likeness of sinful flesh and for sin..." (Rom. 8:3, KJV). He knew no sin (see 2 Cor. 5:21). Christ came for sin as a sin offering. He condemned sin by assuming our sin on the cross. Sentence was passed and executed on sin in Christ's flesh. Those who are "in Christ" have identified with Him in His condemnation of sin in the flesh, and in so doing, have taken the first step to living free of it's dominion.

God's redeeming grace has two aspects. One, grace is God's power for us, the works of pardon and justification through atonement by the Son. Second, grace is also God's power in us, the work of sanctification by the Spirit of God, as well as the Spirit's

21

work in drawing us to repentance and transforming us. As God's power in us, *grace gives us strength to be what we cannot be in ourselves.* The Spirit empowers us to act ethically, including social action, as grace "reigns through righteousness for eternal life" (Rom. 5:21).

> The obedience invoked by what God is and does is not dependent upon our wills alone, for God works in us through both our will and our actions for God's own purpose (Phil. 2:11-12)."[xix]

Christian holiness is not a matter of painstaking conformity to the specific precepts of an external law-code; it is rather a question of the Holy Spirit producing His fruit in our life, reproducing those graces which were seen in perfection in the life of Christ. All that the law required by way of conforming to the will of God is now realized in the lives of those who are controlled by the Holy Spirit and are released from their servitude to the old order. *God's commands have now become God's enablings.*

DIVINE SANCTION - HOLINESS

To fully understand holiness we need to realize that it involves "two sides to the same coin." On one side is God's part in the sanctifying, consecrating process, and on the other hand, man has his important part. God makes us holy (sanctifies us, separates us) (Jn 17:16-17; Heb. 2:11; Eph. 5:25-27; 2 Thess. 2:13b). Man must sanctify himself (set apart, separate) (2 Cor. 7:1; 2 Tim. 2:21; 1 Sam. 16:5; Lev. 11:44; 20:7-8). Isaiah 6:3-7 shows us that God alone is absolute holiness, He only is purely holy. Man is not, inherently. Yet God chooses. God calls. God commissions. Holiness is a gift, an unearned grace-gift from God. God's holiness becomes reality in the people of God (1 Pet. 2:9) by positioning us in Christ. But we can frustrate this gift by corrupting, compromising and conceding to worldly conduct, cultural philosophies, etc.

Therefore, His endowed people, His "holy ones", are not to turn from the life of holiness, but are to continually purge themselves, to "perfect holiness." God has "separated" us by His calling; we must respond by "separating" ourselves from worldly influence. That is our holy calling. That is what holiness is all about."[xx]

God wants to give us power for worthy living (see 1 Thes. 4:7). Jesus' purpose in the incarnation is to "save His people from their sins" (Mt. 1:21). His atonement had in view man's redemption "from every lawless deed and [to] purify for Himself His own special people, zealous for good works" (Tit. 2:14). Its end is not simply deliverance from hell and its misery. It is a rescue and recovery mission where there is an impartation of a holy principle into our lives: restoration of the divine image of purity, reestablishment of communion with the Holy God, ethical recovery and restoration whereby men cease to be and do evil and learn to be and to do good. The life of the Spirit of Christ in the individual believer is the very life of Christ in him reproducing the character of Christ by "forming Christ" within his heart. The holiness of the believer results in fruitfulness, (see Mark 4:26-29).

The nature of the fruit depends on the nature of the parent plant. The spirit-filled life leads to the life of Christ-like conduct. Christ can and does actually give Himself to, share His mind with, put His Spirit into those who really seek the will of God for their lives.

In order to know the will of God, we must have a clear understanding of how God's law relates to us in and through Christ. To make a law legitimate, it must be sanctioned. Sanction can be defined as "the authoritative approval or permission making a course of action valid" and also "a consideration, influence, or principle dictating ethical choice." It can be further defined as "a law or decree; the penalty for noncompliance specified in a law or decree; a penalty, specified or in the form of moral pressure, that acts to ensure compliance or conformity."[xxi]

The significance of the Law is that it inscripturates God's command in propositional form as a fixed rule of life. As such, it is an expression of God's eternal moral will, grounded ultimately in the very being of God. The Law tells what the eternally righteous Creator and Lord requires of His creatures. Since it is based on the nature and purpose of the changeless God, the Law can never be abolished, but remains forever. Not even Christ abrogates the Law taken in this sense, nor is the divine salvation of sinners by grace accomplished in violation of the moral law or in disregard to justice. ...The law in its Mosaic form of administration is fulfilled by Jesus Christ. The Christian is "not under law" (Rom. 6:14; Gal. 5:18), he is "dead to law" (Rom. 7:4, Gal. 2:19), he is "redeemed from under law" (Gal. 4:5). The law as part of the Mosaic economy, whether ceremonial or moral, has no claim against the believer. Its requirements are met for him, and his salvation is secured for him by the merits of Jesus Christ. ...The law itself looks ahead to the moral law inscribed upon the hearts of men by the Spirit of God (Jer. 31:33). The law of Moses was not given as the way of salvation by works; it presupposed the Abrahamic covenant of grace, and it was addressed to the children of promise, to the chosen people. ...The eternal moral law of God is binding on the believer and unbeliever alike.

To the believer, this is not a predicament of terror for the sole reason that the Saviour has met the full demand of the law and is the ground of his salvation. But believer and unbeliever alike are answerable to the divine moral demand. God condemns one because the law's demands are not met by him; He spares the other because they are met in a substitute.[xxii]

God's will expressed through the law can be understood in a threefold purpose: political, spiritual and moral. In the first use...

...the law functions to restrain sin and maintain order in the world. God has ordained earthly government for this purpose (Mt. 22:17-21; Rom. 13:1-7; 1 Tim. 2:1-4; Titus 3:1-11; 1 Pet. 2:13-17). The second use of the law is the proclamation of God's wrath against sin. In this use, the accusing voice of the law works within the sinner to reveal sin and destroy self-righteous pride (Rom. 3:19, 20; 7:7; Gal. 2:19). The ultimate purpose is to bring the sinner to see his need for Christ and to be saved (Gal. 3:23,24; 1 Tim. 2:1-4). The third use of the law applies only to Christians. It is the call to Christians to "put off" the old nature and flee from sin. This use is necessary because Christians are still sinners who are continually tempted to return to the flesh (namely, the rule of self). But this use of the law is only possible because they are reborn with a new nature that delights in the law and desires to be rid of the flesh (Rom. 7:22-25; Col. 3:5-10). This third use is the exhortation to continue in grace, to resist the flesh, and to yield to the Spirit (Rom. 6:12-14; 8:12-14). Inevitably, this exhortation includes moral guidance (Rom. 12:14-13:14; Gal. 5:16-6:2; Eph. 4:25-6:9; Col. 3:5-4:6; 1 Thess. 4:1-8). It also includes the warning that those who return to the flesh, whether in legalistic or lawless ways, "will not inherit the Kingdom of God" (1 Cor. 6:9-10; Gal. 3:1-10; 5:19-21; Eph. 5:5). The moral law is thus valid for the Christian, not as a means of salvation, but as a guide in sanctification.[xxiii]

Thus we conclude that the law was never designed to offer anyone eternal life; it has never been intended to be set in opposition to the promises of God. ...The moral law, as revealed in the Old Testament, was the recognized standard of holiness that remained authoritative for Christ, the apostles, and the early church because it was written. It is proper to speak of the law as being "done away with" or of our having been "set free from" it only in the sense that now in Christ has the law reached its proper end and goal, for He perfectly fulfilled its commands in His life as well as His death.

> Thus, we believers are finished with the law in its ceremonial demands and ceremonial sanctions, but we will continue to find an abiding use for the law in these areas: The moral law continues to function as one of Scripture's formal teachers on what is right and wrong in conduct. The moral law continues to provide standards by which men and women are convinced and convicted of their sin and guilt. We had not known sin, in some cases, except God's law had shown it for what it was. The moral law is a coercive force helping the redeemed to spot moral imperfections that still cling to their lives as they "are being changed from glory to glory."[xxiv]

In following the moral law of God, we have to guard ourselves from a legalistic attitude. A legalist could be described as...

> ...one who adheres rigidly to moral rules and does not exercise sufficient flexibility in the application of those rules to the human situation. ...Often accompanying the use of the term *legalist* is the implicit suggestion that the offending party is not sufficiently motivated by compassion or human concern.[xxv]

> The religious party of the Pharisees, during the time of Jesus, offers a case study in moralistic thinking. Ironically most of the opposition Jesus faced was not pagan but religious. ...The Pharisees advocated a precise and carefully nuanced interpretation of biblical law. Their aim was to apply the law in every conceivable situation. In time, they added to the biblical commands a tradition of by-laws and applications designed to ensure an exacting program of Righteousness. ...It is not difficult to understand why attention shifted from the fundamental concerns of justice,

26

mercy, and faithfulness to the specific details of dietary laws, tithing codes, and Sabbath rules. Obedience was reduced to a measurable performance test. Their zeal for the finer points of the law resulted in the formation of small communities dedicated to preserving their ceremonial purity and tithing obligations. Jesus was a threat to this approach to ethics. He was concerned with divorce, lust, anger, power, wealth, revenge, and lying. The Pharisees were concerned with tithing their spices, keeping up their image, and preserving their national identity. Jesus explored the heart; the Pharisees judged on appearance.[xxvi]

A clearer understanding of how we are to follow the law of God and not enter into legalism would come as a result of understanding the difference between laws, principles and rules. From the transcultural, unalterable, universal laws which God has given, we develop principles. Principles are guidelines for action based on a synthesis of the collected body of information or teaching related to a specific law.

Principles are drawn from three or four passages of God's Word because God's Word does not always have a specific law laid out for every action. Six hundred and thirteen laws were given to the Jewish people. These were later reduced in essence to three: love, justice and to show mercy. Christ ultimately brought them down to one: "You shall love the Lord your God with all your heart and your neighbor as yourself." This became the law. Paul said: "By love serve one another." In essence, the whole law can be reduced to one word: love. From the law, the law of love, we get principles for living. From principles we develop rules.

Rules are guidelines for individual or corporate arrangements to assist individuals in fulfilling principles or laws. Rules may be culturally oriented.

Rules are usually based on an effort to fulfill the Spirit of the principle or the law.[xxvii]

Our confusion comes when we elevate our rules to an equal value with the laws that God has revealed. We cannot possibly interpret God's law apart from God's Spirit. God's law expresses to us His love. It provides for us a pathway to freedom and wholeness. The commandments were not given to limit our freedom or focus on punishment. They were given to point the pathway to purposeful living and fulfillment. The same God who spoke the commandments spoke through Jesus when He said, "I have come that they might have life, and that they may have it more abundantly" (Jn 10:10).

The Commandments are laws of love and relationships that lead us to responsible behavior. The principles of these laws lead us to a loving relationship with God and with each other. We receive the affirmation and acceptance of being children of God. Through these principles we have direction for making right choices, for it is the choices we make in life that affect our happiness or unhappiness, not only in this world, but the world to come.

Clearer understanding of what God is like is learned through His commandments. They teach us what it means to be human. Only humans can disobey God. Also, only humans can willingly choose to obey God. Within the realm of our possibilities are both obedience and disobedience. Our choice, a result of our inner thinking, finds its outward expression in what we say and in our actions (see Prov. 23:7; Jn 7:38).

The Ten Commandments pertain to the very foundations of our personal lives. We are free to choose. The exercise of that freedom, however, does have consequences. We are free to say "yes" or "no" to God, but our lives reveal the consequences of those choices. No one really "breaks" the commandments. If we are disobedient, they break us. We live in a universe governed by laws. If we step off a roof, we fall victim to the law of gravity. Moral and spiritual laws also must be followed, or we fall victim to their consequences. For every action, there is a reaction. God has given guides so that we may find freedom, love, meaning and purpose. God's commandments are meant to be a light for our journey. Psalm 119:105 states, "Your Word is a lamp to my feet and a light to my path."

> God's commandment, revealed in Jesus Christ, embraces the whole of life. It does not only, like the ethical, keep watch on the untransgressible frontier of life, but it is at the same time the center and the fulness of life. ...It becomes the element in which one lives without always being conscious of it, and, thus it implies freedom of movement or of action, freedom from the fear of decision, freedom from fear to act, it implies certainty, quietude, confidence, balance and peace.[xxviii]

Part of the majesty and mystery of our humanity is that God created us capable of choice and He wants us to choose life by choosing Him, His way and His will. But the choice is always ours.

DIVINE MISSION - WITNESS

Jesus, before ascending into Heaven, left His followers with a vision and a command to carry out. "Go into all the world," He charged them, "and preach the Gospel to every creature" (Mk 16:15). They would have the promise of the Father-the Holy Spirit-to enable them to complete this divine mission, that the words spoken by the prophet Isaiah might be fulfilled: "...all the ends of the earth shall see the salvation of our God." (Is. 52:10). The challenge for these men, as Jesus poured out His Spirit and gave birth to the Jerusalem church, was to structure this body of believers in such a way as to be able to fulfill this mandate. A proper structuring of the church was needed in order for the gospel to be carried to a lost world. It had to be based upon a divine pattern and blueprint.

This divine pattern is something that is revealed through the Word of God, by the Spirit of God, in the timing of God. God spoke to Ezekiel to make known to the people of Israel the "law of the temple" (see Ezek. 43:10-12): instruct them in its design, its arrangements, its exits and entrances, all its laws. He further instructed him to write it down so that they could keep its whole design, its ordinances, and perform them.

The Lord also spoke to Habbakuk, the prophet, and instructed him to "Write the vision and make it plain on tablets, that he may run who reads it. For the vision is yet for an appointed time; but at the end it will speak, and it will not lie. Though it tarries, wait for it; because it will surely come, it will not tarry." (Hab. 2:2-3).

The book of Proverbs tells us something about vision, or in some cases the lack of it. "Where there is no vision the people are unrestrained..." (Prov. 29:18, NAS). Unrestrained people are like a stampede of wild horses running in all directions, each one having different ideas about what to do and how to do it. One pulls towards his favorite idea and another pulls in the opposite direction. Too many visions having little relationship with God's overall vision causes the Church to lose direction and destiny.

We find that the Old Testament temple was a type of the New Testament Church, a called-out community of God's people, which is being built on a foundation which Includes the apostles and prophets with Jesus Christ, Himself, being the Chief Cornerstone. In Him the whole building is joined together to grow into a holy temple in the Lord for a habitation of God in the Spirit.

God's vision is plain: Christ is the builder, working in His people by the indwelling of the Holy Spirit to build His Church, to accomplish His Father's vision and bring glory to Him. The Church was not to be a mere religious organization based upon outward conformances, but a corporate expression of Christ's life working within His many- membered body.

30

God's three-fold vision then is that we be individually and personally conformed to Jesus Christ, knowing Him and being like Him in all things; that all believers in Christ be in complete unity in the bonds of covenant love; and that the gospel be preached to all men in every nation on earth.

God's vision gave birth to His mission that was to have a people become a witness to His rule. God's will was to bring unity to all of life. He revealed Himself through the law and the prophets and more fully through His Son, Jesus. Through the sinless life of Christ and His death, burial, and resurrection we can have forgiveness of sins and the enabling power of the Holy Spirit to walk holy before Him. Now He calls us not only individually, but corporately, to become a community which is visible, rather than obscure. We are called to accomplish a task-discipleship with a purpose.

Jesus revealed the nature of the witness we are to have as His disciples in this world in His discourse, the Sermon on the Mount. As a witness, there must be a revelation to the world. We must be seen. We are the light of the world (Mt. 5:14). Light must shine. It's the nature of light to be seen. Light is a positive, aggressive force combatting darkness. It's a force of justice and triumph. Light is a service for those who, having eyes to see, need the path to their destiny illuminated.

Light is also a symbol of salvation and life. Believers are the only ones who can show the world the way to salvation. They are called to demonstrate what God can do in a transformed life. To remain invisible would be a denial of the call of God. A community that hides has ceased to follow the Lord. Jesus hammered home this point by likening this community to "a city set on the hill." A city is made up of people, functioning under a government, with a particular identity that distinguishes it from other cities. God's people are to be an example of a body wherein the rule of God is present and His light seen.

Jesus also likened His people to salt. Salt is both a preserver and a flavoring agent. It is a most indispensable necessity of life. It symbolized the strength and truthfulness of the people's self-surrender as they declared their loyalty, dependence on God, and willingness to serve Him (see Lev. 2:13). The disciples of the Lord are of supreme value to the world, without which it could not live. Their lives are to be a sustaining power on the earth. Only as salt retains its cleansing and flavoring properties can salt preserve the earth. Salt must remain salt. We must remain faithful to the mission to which Christ has called us. But how is this body made visible?

Let's look at the commissioning process given in Matthew 28: 19-20. First we are told to make disciples, then baptize them in Christ, and finally to teach them to observe all commands. This reveals the responsibility of the discipling church as it goes out to fulfill the commission of the Lord. First, we must make the lost into disciples of or learners of Christ, then we bring them to a decision to being identified with Christ and immersed into Christ. Finally, we give them instruction in the commandments of the Lord, including how to relate to the new community of believers.

This divine pattern can be seen in the Book of Acts 2:38-41. Peter preached the first message of the early Church following Pentecost, when those gathered in the upper room were filled with the Holy Spirit. The outcome was that those who received His word were baptized, and were added. To what were they added? They were added to the Church (see Acts 2:47). Note what followed as the Church continued in the apostles teachings.

The apostles were men chosen by God to bear witness to the events of His revelation in Jesus Christ. They were eyewitnesses (see 1 John 1:1-4), foundation builders (Eph. 2:20), carrying the Word of God, not the word of men (1 Thes. 2:13). The sum of the apostles' teaching was "Christ in His Church."

In the life of the Church, one cannot separate the individual disciple from the Body of Jesus. In the Christian life, they belong inseparably together (see Acts 2:42). The infant church of Acts 2 was a visible community which all the world could see. They had "favor with all the people" (Acts 2:47). The Lord added to them day by day those that would be saved. The daily growth of the Church is the proof of the power of the Lord Who dwells in it.

Everything the disciple does is, or should be, part of the common life of the church of which he is a member. There is no department of life in which the members may withdraw from the Body, nor should we desire to withdraw. It is our baptism into the Body of Christ which assures us of a full share in the life of Christ and the Church. When a man is baptized into the body of Christ, not only is his personal status in regard to salvation changed, but also the relationship of daily life. In baptism, we are grafted into the vine of the Lord. This involves a cutting away of our former position and a grafting into a new state. The seal of this baptism is the Holy Spirit, who confirms that the transplanted branch has taken hold of its new position in Christ. It is through this new relationship that the believer will grow and prosper in the fruit of God's Spirit. Whatever we are, whatever we do, everything happens in the Body, in the Church, in Christ. This is how the Church invades the life of the world and conquers territory for Christ. The member in the Body of Christ has been delivered from the world and called out of it; He must give the world a visible proof of his calling.

If we are to be both salt and light, then we must exhibit the purity of the Lord's holiness, while at the same time being an example of God's love. The early church continued in the apostles' doctrine and had all things in common.

Note that the commandments given to the apostles were meant to be taught to a body of believers. The purity that needed to be exhibited by Christ's followers was not something that they could manufacture nor complete through observance. Only through baptism into the Body of Christ and the baptism of the Holy Spirit could the believer have the power necessary to overcome sin in his life. The body of believers are to encourage each other in covenant love to the holiness of God.

There is a need for the simultaneous practice of two biblical principles. The first is the principle of the practice of purity of the visible church. The scriptures teach that we must practice, not just talk about, the purity of the visible church. The second is the principle of an observable love and oneness among all true Christians. The mark of a Christian stresses from John 13:34,35 that according to Jesus Himself, the world has the right to decide whether we are true Christians, true disciples of Christ, on the basis of the love we show to all true Christians. John 17:21 provides something even more sobering in that Jesus gives the world the right to judge whether the Father has sent the Son on the basis of whether the world sees observable love among all true Christians.

One cannot explain the explosive dynamite, the *dunamis*, of the early church apart from the fact that they practiced two things simultaneously: orthodoxy of doctrine and orthodoxy of community in the midst of the visible church, a community which the world could see. By the grace of God, therefore, the church must be known simultaneously for its purity of doctrine and the reality of its community.

We have, then, two sets of parallel couplets: (1) the principle of the practice of the purity of the visible church, and yet the practice of observable love among all true Christians; and (2) the practice of orthodoxy of doctrine and observable orthodoxy of community in the visible church.

The heart of these sets of principles is to show forth the love of God and the holiness of God simultaneously. If we show either of these without the other, we exhibit not the character, but a caricature of God for the world to see. If we stress the love of

34

God without the holiness of God, it turns out to be a compromise. But if we stress the holiness of God without the love of God, we practice something that is hard and lacks beauty. ...In the name of our Lord Jesus Christ, we are called upon to show a watching world and to our young people that the church is something beautiful.[xxix]

The human body is God's masterpiece in creation (Gen. 1:26-28 2:7; Ps. 139:13-17). With its untold millions (perhaps 30-50 million) of cells, etc., its marvelous nervous system of communication, the blood, the skin, the arms and legs and feet, the heart, liver, kidneys, lungs, brains, head, eyes, ears, the protective structure of the bones (at least 246 bones in the body - 63 in the head, 24 in the sides, 16 in the wrist, 14 in the joints, 108 in the hands and feet), etc., and the wonder of all these working together in marvelous harmony and unity in the one body of man - all is indeed the marvel of the divine creation.

If God did this in the old creation man, what shall He do in the new creation man - the body of Christ? He desires to relive His life in the Church which is His body. There are millions of unseen members in the natural body, as well as the seen. Yet all work together in harmony for a whole and healthy body. The unseen and visible members and cells maintain the seen and visible in active health and life. There are no "independent" members in the body. Every joint supplies (see Eph. 4:16).[xxx]

Because of the unique purpose which God has made known, because of the tremendous plan God has for the Body and because of the intricate interrelationships in the Body, no true believer can find fulfillment and accomplishment outside the Body of Christ, the Church. Just as Christ's natural body was visible, even so His present Body has its visible expression. To fail to identify with the visible Body of Christ or the local church is to sever yourself from the Body. As soon as you cut off your foot, that foot loses its function.

The foot only has a function as it relates to the body. Our ministries are only useful or edifying to the Body as they are properly related to the Body. When they are properly related, the life-giving blood will flow to cleanse, heal and nourish each and every member of the Body.

There is something even more severe if we cut ourselves off from the Church, the Body of Christ. When a person rejects the Body, he rejects the Head. A severed foot no longer responds to the commands and directions of the brain. When a person rejects the Body, he rejects God's chain of command and becomes a law unto himself. This is lawlessness. God calls it rebellion.

There are many today who desire to be used of God, but they refuse to come under the authority of the Body of Christ. When we understand what the Body means to God, it is not hard for us to see why rebellion is condemned so harshly by Him (Is. 1:19-23; 1 Sam 15:23; Prov. 17:11; Jer. 28:16; Ps. 68:6; Mt. 7:21-23).

> God gives us strict instructions not to forsake the assembling of ourselves together. As we gather as the Body of Christ, we will be strengthened, the Body will be built up and the purpose of God will be accomplished in and through Christ's Body, the Church.[xxxi]

We must maintain a balanced view of the Church's purpose.

> For the church to have a corrective impact on the culture it must maintain a separate and distinct identity from the surrounding society and any new society that it may help to create. Mission is consistent with separation as long as it is kept in mind that the motivation for that separation is mission, and not separation for its own sake. The only way to really retain true spiritual values is to quicken them with the divine imperative of witnessing to the world. This dynamic nonconformity finds its base in scripture (rather than in the culture of two generations ago) and those who

36

live by it will be enabled to give moral and spiritual direction to the world."[xxxii]

DIVINE PREPARATION - FAITHFULNESS (BRIDE)

The revelation given to Paul concerning the Church as the great mystery, the Bride of Christ, shows the ultimate intention of the Lord for His Church (Eph. 5:23-32). This is Godward in its truth even as the earlier revelations were outward and inward in their truths.

The Church is to be: *A sanctified Church that is holy, separated unto the Lord; a cleansed Church, by the washing of water by the Word; a glorious Church, clothed with glory and bringing glory to Christ; a Church without spot or wrinkle, even as the Old Testament sacrifices were to be without spot, wrinkle, blemish or any such thing; a holy Church, separated from sin; a Church like unto Christ so that He can be united to her and not have a unequal yoke in this marriage.*

> The word has gone forth out of the mouth of the Lord and the zeal of the Lord of Hosts will perform it (Isaiah 55:9-11).
>
> This is the kind of church He will have."[xxxiii]

Throughout scripture there is a special relationship between God and His people. God likens this relationship to a marriage where He is the husband and Israel His wife (see Jer.14).

The great mystery of which Paul speaks is Christ becoming the divine Bridegroom and the Church His Bride.

When you examine the New Testament, you find that the brideship is thought of in two ways. In some places the emphasis is upon the fact that each Christian is, individually, the Bride of Christ, and in other places it is the church as a entity that is the Bride of Christ. But there is no contradiction in this; there is merely unity in the midst of diversity. The church is collectively the Bride of Christ, and it is made up of individual Christians, each one of whom is the Bride of Christ. [xxxiv]   John the Baptist testified of Jesus as the Bridegroom (see Jn. 3:28,29). The relationship of Christ and His Church (His people) is described in terms of the covenant of marriage with Christ being the husband and the Church, His wife.

Furthermore, the apostle Paul describes the relationship of the believer to Christ in these terms: "Therefore, my brethren, you also have become dead to the law through the body of Christ, that you may be married to another, even to Him who was raised from the dead, that we should bear fruit to God"(Rom. 7:4).

In order to understand the relationship we have by being married to Christ, we must compare the relationship God's people had with the law in terms of a marriage relationship.

Those people who see their hope of being justified centered in their relationship to the law do not have happy marriages to the law. Married as they are to the law which is perfect, inflexible, demanding, and all-encompassing, they are soon driven to despair by their own incapability, in the same way that tender young brides have been known to be destroyed by domineering husbands whose rectitude was matched only by their insensitivity. Paul outlined something of the pressures experienced by the brides of the law when he wrote, "Cursed is every one that continueth not in all things which are written in the book of the law to do them"' (Gal. 3:10).

> If we may take the marriage analogy a little further, we can imagine what it must be like for a bride to be confronted each day by a husband who has a list of things which must be done thoroughly and perfectly. She must continue to do them; she must not only think about them but actually perform them. No half measures will be tolerated; no concessions to weakness will be made. There will be no excuses, no explanations will be asked for or given, and every failure in every case will result in the unfortunate bride being cursed for her ineptitude and incompetence. To add

38

insult to injury, the enraged husband will then proceed to live in total inflexible adherence to his own impossible demands, humiliating the bride even more. ...His exemplary behavior is a witness to the perfection of his own demands but also to the imperfection of her abilities. The resultant breakdown of relationship reaches culmination when, upon the death of Mr. Law, the bride breathes more sighs of relief than she sheds tears of remorse. No longer must she embark each morning on an impossible task, knowing full well that she must face each evening the inevitable condemnation of Mr. Perfection. She is free![xxxv]

Max Lucado describes...

...a story of a woman who for years was married to a harsh husband. Each day he would leave her a list of chores to complete before he returned at the end of the day. "Clean the yard. Stack the firewood. Wash the windows... ." If she didn't complete the tasks, she would be greeted with his explosive anger. But even if she did complete the list, he was never satisfied; he would always find inadequacies in her work. After several years, the husband passed away. Some time later she remarried, this time to a man who lavished her with tenderness and adoration. One day, while going through a box of old papers, the wife discovered one of her first husband's lists. And as she read the sheet, a realization caused a tear of joy to splash on the paper. "I'm still doing all these things, and no one has to tell me. I do it because I love him."[xxxvi]

"Life under the law is a never-ending list of rules and regulations which produce a never-ending stream of fears and frustrations. But marriage to Christ is a relationship of love which freely submits and obeys with delight."[xxxvii]

Having been raised from the dead, He will die no more

(Romans 6:9); therefore this new marriage relationship will not be broken by death, as the old one was. ...The fruit of the marriage is a new life, characterized by good works, which God prepared beforehand, that we should walk in them (Eph. 2:10).[xxxviii]

These works are not the means to justification, but simply the response of a bride displaying her love for her bridegroom, resulting in fruitfulness.

The love of Christ for His church revealed in this figure (bride) is an outstanding demonstration of the love of God. Five characteristics of divine love may be mentioned. (1) The eternal duration of the love of God stems from the fact that "God is love" (1 John 4:8). (2) The love of God is the motivation for His ceaseless activity. (3) The love of God has transparent purity. (4) The love of God has limitless intensity (Rom. 8:39). (5) The love of God has inexhaustible benevolence.[xxxix]

God's love can be understood further in this analogy of marriage. Think of all the preparations that a bride makes in order to present herself to her husband in all her beauty.

She wants to be seen lovely and in splendor, without spot or wrinkle or any such thing. So the church is to appear before her heavenly bridegroom (Rev. 21:2). But the difference in this case is that she can do nothing of herself to make herself beautiful in the eyes of her Lord. Of necessity it is all His work. He must thus present the church to Himself. The word translated *in splendor (endoxon)* speaks of honor, of glory, of beauty, but it is implied that the church owes "all her glory to His work." She can only be *without spot or wrinkle*, the stains of sin, and the decadence of age, through what is effected by His sanctifying and renewing work.[xl]

In this relationship the bride needs to be found faithful. Anything that is apart from faith is sin. The bride is called to be a virgin and given only to one. Throughout scripture there are contrasting themes of the true and the apostate; the pure virgin and the harlot woman. In contrast with Israel, who is the unfaithful wife of Jehovah, the Church is pictured in the New Testament as the virgin bride awaiting the coming of her Bridegroom (see 2 Cor. 11:2). The uniting of man and woman in marriage is a picture of the intentions of God in the relationship of Christ and the Church.

> Marriage among the Jews of Paul's day involved two separate ceremonies, the betrothal and the nuptial ceremony which consummated the marriage. Usually a year elapsed between the two, but during that period the girl was regarded legally as the man's wife, while socially she remained a virgin. The betrothal contract was binding, and could be broken only by death or a formal written divorce. Unfaithfulness or violation of a betrothed girl was regarded as adultery and punishable as such. ...Paul sees himself as the agent of God through whom his converts were betrothed to Christ, and feels under obligation to ensure that they are presented as a pure virgin to her one husband at the nuptial ceremony when the marriage will be consummated (2 Cor. 11:2-3).[xli]

"There is a place for a spiritual father's passionate concern for the exclusive and pure devotion to Christ of his spiritual children, and also a place for anger at potential violators of that purity (2 Cor. 11:29)."[xlii] Paul was warning the Corinthian church that they needed to produce fruit likened to the bridegroom or else they were being unfaithful. What is wrong when the right kind of fruit is not being grown (see Rom. 7:4)? The branch must be abiding in the wrong tree (see Rom. 6:13-21).

> There are reasons why we may not be bringing forth the fruit we should. It may be because of ignorance, because we

41

may never have been taught the meaning of the work of Christ for our present lives. There are five possible "ignorances" in this area. First, the Christian may have been taught how to be justified, but never taught the present meaning of the work of Christ for him. Second, he may have been taught to become a Christian through the instrumentality of faith, but then he may have been left, as though from that point on the Christian life has to be lived in his own strength. Third, he may have been taught the opposite. That is, that having accepted Christ, in some antinomian way it does not now matter how he lives. Fourth, he may have been taught some kind of second blessing, which would make him perfect in this life when he receives it. This the Bible does not teach. And therefore he just waits hopelessly, or tries to act upon that which does not exist. Fifth, he may never have been taught that there is a reality of faith to be acted on consciously after justification. This last point is the point of ignorance of many who stand in the orthodox and historic stream of the Reformation.

Because of any of these ignorances, the Christian may not "possess his possessions" in this present life. But when a man does learn the meaning of the work of Christ in the present life, a new door is open to him. And this new door then seems to be so wonderful that often it gives the Christian, as he begins to act upon the knowledge of faith, the sense of something that is as new as was his conversion.[xliii]

As we continue to act upon the knowledge of faith, we begin to make wise, ethically-sound decisions that honor God and produce the fruit of our union. The fruit of the heart that follows after God will be expressed in the decisions, priorities, and activities of daily life. Perhaps the most realistic life-example of applied wisdom is

42

the description by the writer of Proverbs of a person who feared the Lord and whose life-pattern displayed this characteristic.

It is the description of the Proverbs 31 woman.

The character of this noble woman shines through all the activities of her busy life. The quality of her character cannot be measured by an itemized list of activities nor is the beauty of her character judged by cosmetic charm. She is wise in the depth of her being because she fears the Lord. She surpasses women who do "noble things" and her beauty does not fade with age. The closest to her see in her an example of God's grace and strength. Her family benefits from her confidence, discernment, and diligence. She has exchanged the flattery of superficial compliments for the praise of her character. This woman desires and demonstrates a discerning heart in everything she does.

Her life exemplifies the multifaceted nature of true wisdom; it touches every area of life. She can work with her hands as well as with her mind. She is active in the home and outside the home. She cares for her family materially and spiritually. Yet she does not live entirely for her family. She gives to the poor and needy as well. There is consistency and a coherence to her lifestyle. She is balanced but not bored, active but not hassled. She lives without excuses. Her spirituality is woven into the fabric of her life. She refuses to compartmentalize her activity into spiritual and secular categories. Her Mondays are as holy as her Sabbaths.

All we see in this woman of noble character presents a beautiful portrait of wisdom's harmony. She is fulfilled within herself but not by herself. She is one with her husband and supportive of her children. Her life in all its dimensions is its own reward! She is worthy of praise. But her real reward is in her work, in her relationships, in the experience of God's wisdom in her life. She does not do things to get them over

43

with so she can get on with her own life. Her fear of the Lord and humble service to the poor save her from self-righteousness.[xliv]

This is not a picture of any woman, but a picture of the bride of Christ- one who has made herself ready. And it is granted to her to be arrayed in fine linen, clean and bright, for the fine linen is the righteous acts of the saints (see Rev. 19:7-8).

The Bridegroom spoke the words of wisdom in the Sermon on the Mount. He began with the beginning of wisdom, the fear (worshipping submission) of the Lord (see Mt. 5:3), and ended with how a wise man builds (see Mt. 7:24-27). Within the context of this Scripture, Jesus expounded on how a disciple's righteousness needs to exceed a mere outward observance (see Mt. 5:20). One's conceptual knowledge of God would be united with the experiential knowledge of God, which would produce a spiritual life that would be centered on the Word of God. The end picture of wisdom was revealed as the Church, the bride, a spiritual house, where wisdom hewed out her seven pillars (see Prov. 9:1); where the image of the visible Christ comes and challenges us to live in unity, forgiven that we might become holy, obedient (an example to others), and faithful.

> The fundamental dynamics of how to make moral choices are the same today as they were 2,000 or 3,000 years ago. ...Perhaps it would help to point out the four levels on which the Bible can relate to issues that you face. The first level is *prohibitions:* instructions that are clear and straight-foward, apply directly and unequivocally to specific areas of life, and state mostly in the negative, in terms of what you must not do. "You shall not murder" (Ex. 20:13) is an example of a biblical prohibition.
>
> A second level has to do with the Bible's *positive commands.* These are easy to understand and speak to

44

broad, general areas of behavior. Applying them to a specific situation may take some thought and creativity. "Walk in love" (Eph. 5:2) is a positive command. So is "Husbands, love your wives, just as Christ also loved the church" (Eph. 5:25).

A third level of biblical instruction is **values and principles** (Principles are basic truths taught by the Bible that apply to life). The fourth level is the area of **conscience**. Matters of conscience occur when there are no clear prohibitions of Scripture that apply unequivocally to a situation. Instead, you have to forge a response out of whatever positive commands and principles you believe apply. In this area God leaves you with a great deal of latitude in what you decide to do. Applying these four levels of biblical instruction to life is what the Bible calls *wisdom,* which literally means "the skill of living."[xlv]

Skill takes time to develop; however, the Holy Spirit will enable us to discern truth, as we apply the Word of God to our lives. This produces a freedom in us and allows us to align our words with our deeds, while we give God the allegiance of our hearts. Therefore, the ultimate ethical purpose is fulfilled - the praise of God. God is praised as His will is done. Obedience is the means to achieve this goal. The grace of God empowers us to fulfill our moral imperative.

CONCLUSION

The word *ethics* comes from the Greek *ethos* meaning "foundation" or "root" and has to do with the philosophical basis for morality. It encompasses the reasons why certain behavioral patterns are perceived or accepted as more appropriate than others. Unlike morality which is concerned with what is actually taking place, ethics focuses on what ought to be done. Since the Christian perspective holds that people are required to do what they ought to do, what they ought to do is being determined by God, the distinction between ethics and morality is significant for the Christian. A Christian's moral acts should be defined by a Godly ethics, which are Christ-centered.

The fact that God is righteous - or always "in the right" - is both a challenge and a comfort. The challenge comes to mankind through the realization that the rightness of human action must be determined not by the fluctuating moral standards of a volatile society, but by the unchanging revelation of an eternal God. The comfort of knowing that God is always "in the right" is found in the experience of the humble person who, though inconsistently turning to the Lord for wisdom when surrounded by an endless stream of contradictions, does turn and discovers that truth can be known and that right still exists.

This comfort, however, is frequently short-lived because the chasm that emerges between knowing what is right and doing what is right is oftentimes vast. The closer a man gets to the righteousness of God, the more uncomfortable he becomes about his own righteousness. In our search for truth, we see how unable we are to live it, and we either deny what is right because we can't live it in our own strength, or we turn to the enablement of God and try to live it - we run the race.

The gospel, however, recognizes this and in its revelation of the righteousness of God, shows how the one who is not "in the right" before God can have his situation rectified. Through a transforming process, man is restored to the image of God through an obedience to the will of God that enables man to be brought into a relationship with God. Out of this relationship come direction, destiny, and the enablement to fulfill that destiny. Ultimately, God is praised, which is the goal of all human conduct. God is praised as His will is done. Obedience is thus the means to achieve the goal, and a relationship with God is the means through which we achieve obedience.

Nevertheless, God's glory does not remain alone, for the glory of God means also the glorifying of the creature (see Rom. 8:17, 30; 2 Cor. 3:18), a demonstration of His ongoing love for us. This glorifying is linked with the "spirit of sonship" that is given to all children of God, who by faith are joined to Christ (Rom. 8:15-17) through the cross. Human beings are thus brought into union with God both *in being and in act* - a union that embraces union with fellow believers (see Eph. 4:4-16). In the obedient doing of the will of God, one achieves the authentic humanity, or being, in the divine image, which God planned for men and women in His creative work. Since the divine mandate at creation included dominion over other creatures (see Gen. 1:26), the proper ordering and curatorship of the physical environment forms part of theological ethics in accordance with its goal in God (see Rom. 8:18-22).

In regard to our goal, as well as ground, norm, and power, Holy Scripture plays a key role, for it is only through the inspired record of God that God, as the goal of human action, may be known and accepted, with all that this implies for the direction of the life, the course and validity of right action, and the destiny of those who commit themselves to God as their all in all.

Finally truth, as revealed by God, requires wisdom in its application. Tension is needed to hold onto truth. At the extremes we find legalism and antinomianism; either side is error. As we discern truth, we must search out its foundation, the seed from which it was brought forth, as well as looking at the results or fruit that a truth has produced. Man's desire to walk in truth is reflective of God's creative work. God, who is truth, created man in His image to reflect truth in his daily walk. Man was to know truth through his experiential relationship with God (e.g., God and Adam walking together in the cool of the day - what experience were they sharing?) and not by thoughts and reasonings exclusive of God. With this in mind, we hide the Word of God in our heart, for it is a light unto our path. The Word of God directs our experiential walk with God. The more the truth of the Word is revealed, the more we can experience God who is truth; the more we experience the truth, the closer we come to our quest - not only to know truth, but to walk in truth. Let us continue to walk in the light of the narrow road prepared for us.

CHAPTER 2
FOUNDATIONS FOR MINISTERIAL ETHICS

MINISTERIAL INTEGRITY

Ministerial ethics begins with ministerial integrity, which can be defined as "completeness" or "wholeness." Jesus captures the gospel sense of integrity with the command, *"Be perfect as your heavenly Father is perfect"* (Matt. 5:48). In the English text, "perfect" renders the Greek word *teleios,* which means "complete." This teaching concludes Jesus' authoritative interpretation of the Law *("You have heard that it was said. . . But I say to you"),* which in turn interprets the Sermon's theme, *"unless your righteousness exceeds that of the scribes and Pharisees, you will never enter the kingdom of heaven"* (Matt. 5:20). Integrity in the gospel sense entails being completed or formed by the Word of God which comes to us in Jesus Christ. Jesus' conclusion to the Sermon suggests that such integrity is the embodiment of wisdom:

> *Everyone then who hears these words of mine and act on them will be a wise man who built his house on rock. The rain fell, the floods came, and the winds blew and beat on that house, but it did not fall, because it had been founded on rock. And every one who hears these words of mine and does not act on them will be like a foolish man who built his house on sand. The rain fell, and the floods came, and the winds blew and beat against that house; and it fell-and great was its fall!* (Matt. 5:24-27)

The reaction to those who heard the Sermon connects integrity to the life-changing impact of gospel truth: *"Now when Jesus had finished saying these things, the crowds were astonished at His teaching, for He taught them as one having authority, and not as their scribes"* (Matt. 5:28-29). We begin to have integrity in the gospel sense when we hear and follow Jesus on our way to becoming a truthful people. Receiving, embodying, and telling the truth of God in Christ is the essence of ministerial integrity. Indeed, the failure of ministerial integrity is in large measure the failure to know and bear witness to this very truth.

The church is complicit in the loss of ministerial integrity. We live in a consumer society, and churches routinely function as subsets of this society. We come to church as individuals with needs, and we expect our ministers to meet our needs. We feel guilty, and we need forgiveness. We feel lonely, and we need companionship. We feel grief, and we need to be comforted. We feel depressed, hopeless, empty, alienated, trapped, or aimless, and we need encouragement, assurance, reconciliation, liberation, and direction. We feel bored, and we need to be entertained. Sensitive to our needs, ministers try to meet them, offering absolution, friendship, understanding, motivation, and spiritual inspiration.

While congregants' needs are heart-felt, and ministers' attempts to meet them are genuine, the consumer approach to church and ministry undermines ministerial integrity. Christian ministry is not first and foremost about identifying and meeting the needs of people, but about leading people to follow Jesus and thus to become the people of God. Following Jesus, we are called to be the salt of the earth and the light of the world, to love our enemies, to be agents of reconciliation, to do justice for "the least of these," to love God as we love one another, to serve God as we serve one another, and to bear witness to the cosmos-shaking reality that *"the Word became flesh and lived among us . . . full of grace and truth"* (John 1:14).

When the task of ministry becomes defined by something less than helping the people of God to be formed by the way of Jesus, ministerial integrity is bound to suffer. That is not to deny the clear connection between human needs and Christian ministry, but rather to give an account of what it means to lose (and to regain) ministerial integrity:

> Only a few months into his first pastorate, the new pastor realizes that people's needs are virtually limitless, particularly in an affluent society in which there is an ever-rising threshold of desire (which we define as "need"). There is no job description, no clear sense of purpose other than the meeting of people's needs, so there is no possible way for the pastor to limit what people ask of the pastor. Not knowing what they should do, pastors try to do everything and be everything for everybody. The most conscientious among them become exhausted and empty. The laziest of them merely withdraw into disinterested detachment. Not knowing why their pastor is there, the congregation expects the pastor to be and do everything. They become unrealistic critics of the clergy rather than coworkers, fellow truth-tellers.[xlvi]

There are, of course, other expressions of the loss of ministerial integrity, but all involve the same dislocation from the One who centers us and integrates our lives. Ministerial integrity does not originate in the lives of ministers, vocational or otherwise, but in the Word who became flesh and lived among us, from whose "fullness we have all received, grace upon grace" (John 1:14, 16). These God-given graces grant us the truthfulness, courage, constancy, patience, faith, hope, and love required to follow Jesus in Christian ministry.

The integrity which flows from Spirit-gifted virtues is formed or learned in the context of the community of faith. Scripture plays a crucial role in this formative process, teaching congregations and the ministers who serve them to learn and embody the ways of God. The same biblical stories that teach us what God does (God speaks the universe into existence; calls a people out of slavery;

commands them to do justice, love kindness, and to walk humbly; comes among them as Savior and suffering servant; and tabernacles with them as the Spirit of truth) also bear the expectation that we will reflect the ways of God in our common life. We will reflect God's creative Spirit and honor the creation, liberate the oppressed, do justice in the face of injustice, love mercy and practice forgiveness, serve God as we serve one another, speak the truth in love, encourage one another in righteousness and not settle for anything less. As we are committed to follow Jesus in our common life, the community of faith becomes the training ground for the integrity of character which is requisite for ministry.

As ministers of the gospel we have a responsibility both to declare the truth and to live the truth. This involves both our relationship to God and to others. It means living in a way that upholds the ethical standards for conduct that the Bible teaches. In a day when relativism is rampant, the Bible still points us to God's own character as the standard we must, with the help of the Holy Spirit, strive to follow. It is not enough to follow the norms that the world around us accepts as ethical (Matt. 5:46-48). We also have the example of Jesus, and we can learn from the apostles as they followed Him (1 Cor. 4:16-17; 11:1).

To act ethically in a way that pleases God, we must seek to be like the Father, which also means to be like Jesus who reveals the Father (Matt. 11:27). Consider, then, the character of God revealed in the Bible. Holiness and love stand out. God is love by His very nature (1 John 4:8). When Moses repeated the Ten Commandments in Deuteronomy 5:6-21, he went on to say, "Love the LORD your God with all your heart and with all your soul and with all your strength" (Deut. 6:5). Then he added, "These commandments that I give you today are to be upon your hearts" (v. 6). In other words, the Israelites could not even begin to keep the Ten Commandments in a way that pleased God unless their whole being was going out to God in love.

52

The love God wanted was really a response to His love, for He loved them first (Deut. 7:7-8) and showed His love by delivering them out of Egypt by grace through faith. They had shown that faith by obedience as they sacrificed the Passover lamb, sprinkled its blood, and ate it with everyone dressed, packed up, and ready to go. The Book of Hosea demonstrated further that the kind of love God wanted included a loyalty that Israel throughout its history so often lacked.

Our response to His love must also make us a channel of His love to others. In the midst of the Law, God said, "Love your neighbor as yourself" (Lev. 19:18). Then He added, in Leviticus 19:34, "The alien living with you must be treated as one of your native-born. Love him as yourself, for you were aliens in Egypt. I am the LORD your God." Our God is the kind of God who loves foreigners. The Law also called for acts of love, even to an enemy. However, not many accepted the full meaning of love for the neighbor until Jesus made it real through the Parable of the Good Samaritan (Luke 10:25-37). Jesus also demonstrated divine love many times, for example, in Matthew 9:36: "When He saw the crowds, He had compassion on them, because they were harassed and helpless, like sheep without a shepherd." But no one really understood the fullness of God's love or the kind of love He expects us to show until Jesus died on the cross (John 3:16; Rom. 5:8). That same love – shown "while we were still sinners" – makes a full provision available to us that can not only save us, but also see us all the way through to glory as we follow Jesus (Rom. 5:10). Just how necessary it is for believers to show this kind of love is one of the great themes of 1 John.

The Bible, however, does not make God's love central to His character. In Isaiah's inaugural vision, the seraphim ("burning ones") so reflected God's glory they seemed to be on fire. But they did not call out, "Love, love, love." They kept calling to one another: "Holy, holy, holy is the Lord Almighty; the whole earth is full of His glory'" (Isa. 6:3). Holiness is central to God's nature. Even His love works in line with His holiness – as the Cross demonstrated. God could not be true to Himself and simply excuse our sin because of His love. His holiness demanded that the penalty be paid, "for the wages of sin is death" (Rom. 6:23). So Jesus, the sinless Lamb of God, fulfilled the entire sacrificial system, as well as Isaiah 53. He became our substitute and satisfied the holiness of God.

God's holiness must be the standard of our holiness. Isaiah repeatedly calls Him the Holy One of Israel. God commanded Israel to consecrate themselves and be holy because He is holy (Lev. 11:44-45; cf. 20:26). This involves our cooperation with God, Who makes us holy (Lev. 20:7-8).

God's holiness had two aspects. The basic meaning of the Hebrew word for holiness is "separation." On one hand, God is totally separate from all sin and evil – quite unlike the false gods the pagans believed in, gods they thought could swap wives, kill each other, glorify drunken orgies, and do other evil deeds.

The other aspect of God's holiness is related to His faithfulness. He has separated Himself to the carrying out of His great plan of redemption and to the completing of His purpose to bless all the families of the earth (Gen. 12:3). He will bring people from every nation, tribe, people, and language to share His glory and to be with Him forever (1 Thess. 4:16-17; Rev. 7:9).

Jesus demonstrated these two aspects of holiness. He rejected Satan's temptations, using something that is available to us: God's Word (Matt. 4:1-10). He also demonstrated the positive aspect by identifying Himself with us and taking the place of a humble servant of His Father and of God's people. He told His disciples, "You know that the rulers of the Gentiles lord it over them. [That is, they love to play the tyrant and show their authority.] Not so with you. Instead, whoever wants to become great among you must be your servant, and whoever wants to be first must be your slave – just as the Son of Man did not come to be served, but to serve, and to give His life as a ransom for many" (Matt. 20:25-28). Then, in His prayer in the Garden of Gethsemane, He declared His total submission to His Father's will (Matt. 26:39, 42).

So, too, our holiness must have two aspects. We must turn our backs on sin and evil. We must also take up our cross and follow Jesus (Matt. 10:38; 16:24). The latter is what really makes us holy. We can see this illustrated by the holy vessels of the Old Testament tabernacle and temple. They were separated from ordinary use; they could not be used in the homes of the Israelites. But that is not what made them holy. They became holy when they were taken into the temple and used in the worship and service of the Lord. In a similar way, our holiness involves consecration and dedication of ourselves to the worship and service of the Lord.

However, neither our holiness nor our love is a matter of mere human effort. Nor is it merely our human response to God's holy love. Jesus was the divine Helper for His disciples while He was on earth. He restrained them when they wanted to bring fire down from heaven (Luke 9:54-55). He directed them to feed the multitude (Matt. 14:15-21). He gave them authority and power to heal the sick and drive out demons (Matt. 10:1). Then He promised them "another Counselor" (John 14:16). The basic meaning of "Counselor" is simply "Helper," and "another" means "another of the same kind." Thus the Holy Spirit is our Helper; God pours out His "love into our hearts by [His] Holy Spirit" (Rom. 5:5). He does this not simply for us to enjoy, but to make us channels of that Calvary love, that self-giving love that is to extend even to our enemies.

The Holy Spirit also helps us along the highway of holiness. On the one hand, this means He helps us to reject sin and evil and guides us along "the paths of righteousness" (which in Psalm 23:3 could be translated "ruts of righteousness," well used by godly people who have gone before us and well-marked in Scripture).

On the other hand, the Holy Spirit helps us dedicate ourselves to the worship and service of the Lord. He has gifts and ministry for every believer. But the Holy Spirit distributes His gifts not according to our desires, but "just as He determines" (1 Cor. 12:11).

Our part is to be open to the Spirit's guidance and responsive to His promptings. Believers are not to decide on their own what ministry they want to be involved in. Neither do we put one kind of ministry on a higher level, or consider it more important, than others. First Corinthians 12:14-26 emphasizes the importance of each member of the Body and the necessity and value of every ministry, including those that are unseen or in the background.

The Spirit will guide us in many ways. In the Book of Acts, the Holy Spirit used several means. Sometimes He used circumstances, as when the persecution after the stoning of Stephen caused the believers to scatter in all directions, preaching the Word wherever they went (Acts 8:4). Sometimes He sent an angel, as when God wanted Philip to leave the revival in Samaria and go south to the old, deserted Gaza road that practically no one used anymore (Acts 8:26). But when Philip obeyed, he didn't need another angel to tell him to run alongside the chariot of the Ethiopian eunuch: by his initial obedience he had become more sensitive to the voice of the Holy Spirit, and that was all he needed (vv. 29-20).

Sometimes the Lord does use unusual means to turn people around. He did with Saul the persecutor on the Damascus Road (Acts 9:1-6), and even after Saul became the apostle Paul, at Troas, God used an unusual dream to give him the Macedonian call (Acts 16:9-10).

Acts has no formal ending. The acts of the Holy Spirit, along with His guidance and power, are meant to continue today. When we turn to Paul's epistles, we find that each begins with teaching and then goes on to a practical section, where Paul deals with questions and problems that arose in the Early Church. For some of them he had a word from the Lord. That is, he had a saying or teaching of Jesus to answer their questions or their need. In Galatians he lets us know that he learned from Jesus himself the things He did and taught, probably during Paul's three years in Arabia (1:11-12, 15-18). But where Paul did not have a word of Jesus to give the recipients of his letters, he had the inspired word of the Holy Spirit.

Peter's epistles also are full of guidance for every aspect of Christian living. In our day, perhaps 1 Peter 4:19 is appropriate: "Those who suffer according to God's will should commit themselves to their faithful Creator and continue to do good." "Suffer" means to endure. It is the same word used of the sufferings of Jesus. The faithful Creator is the one who made us and who sent His Son to die on the cross. Committing ourselves to Him means taking up our cross daily and following Him. Doing good then means doing the kind of good He did, telling the good news of the gospel, healing the sick, casting out demons, and encouraging people to turn to Jesus. We are to live for Him. This includes acting ethically in all our relationships and in all we do.

THE STEWARDSHIP OF POWER
Biblical Models of Spiritual Authority

The Old Testament instructs fathers to be the priests of the home and calls for both fathers and mothers to teach their children the laws and statutes handed down by God through Moses. But even prior to the giving of the Law, Abraham served as a model in his home in leading the family from Ur of the Chaldees and later interceding for Lot and the cities of Sodom and Gomorrah. What a powerful illustration he left us when he chose the highest ethic of obedience to God: offering up Isaac, contrary to his own good judgment! A further tribute to his domestic leadership is found in Sarah's relationship to him, a model for Christian wives: "Sarah . . . obeyed Abraham and called him her master. You are her daughters if you do what is right and do not give way to fear" (1 Pet. 3:16).

Jacob, his character seriously flawed, had his personality and ethics overhauled by a physical encounter with God. Subsequently, he came to be respected by his sons as not only the head of the family, but also as their spiritual leader. His position of authority over his strong-willed sons was highlighted by the family's departure for Egypt; they accepted his decision to be dependents of Joseph and Pharaoh's court.

In later years, the prophets of the Old Testament exercised ethical and spiritual authority to the extent that kings and noblemen often cowed before them. Saul, even in his backslidden state, had high regard for Samuel. Ahab quailed before Elijah. Nathan could point his finger in David's face and say, "You are the man!" (2 Sam. 12:7). Elisha's instructions to a proud Syrian general had to be obeyed to the letter in order to produce his healing. At the close of the intertestamental period, John the Baptist, fearless preacher of the doctrine of pure ethics, challenged the adulterous King Herod, who revered and feared him. Even following John's martyrdom, the king lived in dread of his memory.

Perhaps the most striking revelation of Christ's authority came from the lips of the centurion, who reasoned that if he, a man of authority, could order men to do his bidding, it would be a small matter for Christ to bring healing to his servant by a spoken word (Matt. 8:8-10). The centurion's comprehension of spiritual authority was hailed by Christ as the greatest example of faith He has seen in all of Israel. It is worth noting that the entire eighth chapter of Matthew, where the centurion's story is recorded, gives us a number of instances where Christ exercised spiritual authority in accord with the highest ethical standard: He used His authority over space in healing the servant who was a distance away (vv. 6-8, 13). He had already taken authority over leprosy, a type of sin (v. 3). He manifested authority over common household illnesses and all types of sickness (vv. 14-16). He amazed His disciples with His control of the stormy winds and seas (vv. 26-27). He shook an entire city by taking command of a host of demons (vv. 28-34).

As the Early Church took form, Peter, whose ethics had been transformed and energized by the power of the indwelling Holy Spirit, became a leader in the Church. Paul had held to an ethical standard that drove him to fight the Church, only to become its representative who would stand before Kings, Roman centurions, and the Church itself. He was persecuted, stoned, and beaten, but his spiritual authority was seldom questioned; it was the authority of the Holy Spirit Himself.

Along with examples of the proper use of authority, the Bible gives some negative instances as well. Saul, Israel's first king, abused the authority invested in the throne. Later David took unethical advantage of his kingly role in his affair with Bathsheba and the murder of her husband. Balaam is a classic example of the false prophet whose scruples would allow him to make merchandise of God's Word. In the New Testament, Simon's code of ethics, developed through years of practicing sorcery, gave him license to offer money in exchange for spiritual authority.

The Minister's Response to the Lordship of Christ

To make the proper use of spiritual authority, ministers must bear in mind their relationship to the true Head of the Church. Christ is Lord over the Church and over the minister. The resurrected Christ has given ministries to the Church. Their function is to lead the saints as they "grow up into Him who is the Head" of the Church (Eph. 4:11-15). Christ's will must remain paramount in the life of the minister and the church.

Any authority that the minister exercises has been given by Christ. First, Christ modeled the ethical use of spiritual power, and then transmitted it by the Spirit to His called ministers. Richard J. Foster in *Money, Sex and Power* points out the sequence:

> Jesus' ministry was marked with authority. Spiritual power and spiritual authority are inseparable. In his Gospel, Mark tells of Jesus' healing of a demon-possessed person, adding that the people "were all amazed, so that they questioned among themselves, saying, 'What is this? A new teaching! With authority he commands even the unclean spirits, and they obey him'" (Mark 1:27). Jesus was not giving a new teaching; he was demonstrating a new power. He not only proclaimed the presence of the kingdom of God, He demonstrated its presence with power.
>
> Now if Jesus had been the only one who exercised the ministry of power, we might be able to dismiss it as the privileged domain of the Messiah, but he delegated this same ministry to others.[xlvii]

This delegation of authority stems from the Lord's initial calling to follow Him in dedicated service. With the calling comes moral and ethical empowerment. The power-laden commission, first verbalized to the disciples, but transmitted to every called minister through the Scriptures, is clear in its ethical intent: "I will give you the keys of the kingdom of heaven; whatever you bind on earth will be bound in heaven, and whatever you loose on earth will be loosed in heaven" (Matthew 16:19). Thus, the minister becomes the ethically authorized instrument through whom the Spirit works "just as He determines" (1 Cor. 12:11).

Empowered by the Spirit, the minister finds a place to function in the body of Christ. The ministry ethics of the members of the Body dictate that there is no hierarchy of power or authority. God has set the members in the Body as has pleased Him. Members that seem less desirable have been given even greater honor than other members. As a result, any glory granted to an individual member of the Body goes directly to God. "He who glories, let him glory in the Lord" (2 Cor. 10:17). In this connection, Erwin W. Lutzer comments:

> The implications for our ministry are obvious. *God's people do not exist for their own benefit but for His benefit.* In our interpersonal relationships, we must remember that we are dealing with God's property, His people redeemed for His own purposes. That's why church leaders are exhorted to humility and not dictatorial leadership: "Therefore, I exhort the elders among you, as your fellow elder, . . . shepherd the flock among you . . . not for sordid gain, but with eagerness; not yet as lording over those allotted to your charge, but proving to be examples to the flock" (1 Peter 5:1-3).[xlviii]

No matter what the relationship of one ministry to another, none will function properly without love. First Corinthians 12, dealing with the ethics of the interaction and ministry of the parts of the Body, leads into chapter 13 where the beautiful work ethic of the Bible, love, is revealed. In essence, this passage makes it clear that if I abuse my spiritual authority by applying it without love, I am nothing and all of my efforts are empty, meaningless, and without reward.

Interpreting Power in the Community of Faith

Life in the Body of Christ inevitably raises power issues, and these issues are central to ministerial ethics. An important scriptural starting point for interpreting power in the community of faith is Philippians 2:1-11:

> **Philippians 2:1-11** (NKJV) [1] Therefore if *there is* any consolation in Christ, if any comfort of love, if any fellowship of the Spirit, if any affection and mercy, [2] fulfill my joy by being like-minded, having the same love, *being* of one accord, of one mind. [3] *Let* nothing *be done* through selfish

ambition or conceit, but in lowliness of mind let each esteem others better than himself. [4] Let each of you look out not only for his own interests, but also for the interests of others. [5] Let this mind be in you which was also in Christ Jesus, [6] who, being in the form of God, did not consider it robbery to be equal with God, [7] but made Himself of no reputation, taking the form of a bondservant, *and* coming in the likeness of men. [8] And being found in appearance as a man, He humbled Himself and became obedient to *the point of* death, even the death of the cross. [9] Therefore God also has highly exalted Him and given Him the name which is above every name, [10] that at the name of Jesus every knee should bow, of those in heaven, and of those on earth, and of those under the earth, [11] and *that* every tongue should confess that Jesus Christ *is* Lord, to the glory of God the Father.

We are arrested, but not surprised, by Paul's counsel to the Philippian church, for it simply captures in an extraordinarily moving way the fundamental truth which pervades the four gospels. *The way of Jesus is the way of the cross, which is not only the center of salvation history, but also the ethical norm of our common life.* Jesus takes up the cross and commands His followers to do likewise. Paul's application of this central truth to the Body of Christ is that we should become servants of one another as Christ has served us.

The faithful memory of this teaching is always critical to congregational life, just as its disregard accounts for many of the saddest moments in church history. The call to servanthood is the high calling of Christ's ministers, paid or unpaid, vocational or volunteer. In Matthew and parallel passages in Mark and Luke, Jesus said we should not "lord it over" one another and that the greatest of God's people must be servants rather than tyrants (Matt. 20:20-28). Jesus' instruction to His disciples suggests that the corporate executive model of the pastorate in which the pastor rules the church fails to appreciate this distinctively Christian sense of leadership. Christian leaders lead by serving. Power in the conventional sense is, in effect, turned on its head, so that the greatness of leadership is not determined by how many lives we control, but by how faithfully we serve each life with whom God has entrusted us.

To confirm this point and to mute our every attempt to revise the meaning of service, Jesus concludes this instruction with the sentence, "*whoever wishes to be first among you must be your slave*" (Matt. 20:27). "Slave" is descriptively clear. Ministers cannot honestly claim to serve congregations by *overpowering* them. According to the gospel, the faithful stewardship of power in congregational life paradoxically entails the renunciation of power. This "revolutionary subordination"[xlix] is ethically normative for the people of God and stands in judgment over the misuse of power in the community of faith. When ministers attempt to create churches in their own image, consider the church's property as their own property, access the church treasury as their own treasury, manipulate church members and church life on behalf of their own self-interest, they violate the Christian stewardship of power.

Positively, Paul exemplifies the meaning of servanthood in ministry as honoring every member of the Body of Christ. Just as the human body consists of many members and thrives on their comprehensive inter-working, so the Body of Christ depends on the collaboration of the diverse spiritual gifts of church members. 1 Corinthians 12:23 presses the implication of a crucial part of Paul's analogy ("*those members of the body we think less honorable we clothe with greater honor*") to mean that we particularly honor the contributions of church members who in conventional thinking might not seem very important. The servant approach to power is unconventional precisely in that it reverses the slope of conventional social stratification, assuming the vantage point of "below" rather "above." Instead of people on top wielding exclusive authority, people on the bottom are invested with authority and significance as well.

In very close context with the call to servanthood in the gospel passages quoted above are other teachings which have implications regarding the stewardship of power. In Matthew 18:15, Jesus instructs His disciples,

> **Matthew 18:15** (NKJV) [15] "Moreover if your brother sins against you, go and tell him his fault between you and him alone. If he hears you, you have gained your brother.

Jesus goes on to say that if the offender refuses the reconciling initiative, the one who has been offended should continue to make reconciling initiatives until the offender *"refuses to listen even to the church."* At that point, the offender should become *"as a Gentile and tax collector,"* that is, the subject of the church's missionary activity. Jesus concludes His instruction with a remarkable statement, *"Truly I tell you, whatever you bind on earth will be bound in heaven, and whatever you loose on earth will be loosed in heaven"* (Matt. 18:18).

Two implications regarding the stewardship of power in Matthew 18:15-20 complement the call to servanthood. First, ministry involves us in reconciling initiatives which many of us would consider risky. Issues (offenses) should not be swept under the rug and forgotten, but faced positively and redemptively. Jesus describes these initiatives as persistent, eventuating in the possible removal of the offender from church membership. Second, the followers of Jesus are invested with the authority to bind or loose, i.e., to hold onto or release offenses, *"for where two or three are gathered in My name, I am there among them"* (Matt. 18:20).

The term "offense" is not defined or qualified and could presumably include moral transgressions as well as personal attacks. The same Jesus, who in the near context of Matthew's gospel issues several calls to servanthood, here instructs His followers to take reconciling initiatives, to be persistent in doing so, and then grants them power to bind and to loose. Clearly, servant ministry requires *courageous leadership.* We tend to avoid the kinds of initiatives prescribed by Jesus exactly because they are risky and may lead to confrontations. But the one who calls us to servant ministry calls us also to congregational leadership, to be good stewards of the very power we possess as ministers, which is the power to claim and reclaim lives in Jesus' name. The sort of leadership and exercise of power prescribed here is not imperial, but distinctively Christian and consistent with the way of the cross. This is not the power of the tyrant who threatens, extorts, and manipulates, but the power of the good shepherd who simply will not give up on lost sheep. To be faithful to Jesus' call to servant ministry is to be willing to be good stewards of the power resident in spiritual leadership.

In the paragraph which follows Jesus' instruction concerning reconciling initiatives, Peter anticipates the church's potential to abuse the authority to bind and loose. He asks Jesus, *"Lord, if another member of the church sins against me, how often should I forgive? As many as seven times?* Jesus replies, *"Not seven times, but I tell you, seventy times seven"* and goes on to tell the story of the unforgiving servant who, though forgiven much, refused to forgive even a little (Matt. 18:21-35). Jesus' clear instruction to Peter is clear also to us. As we exercise the sort of spiritual and pastoral leadership implicit in *"binding and loosing,"* we do so with no less compassion and mercy as the one who calls us to ministry.

The stewardship of power involved in spiritual leadership takes other forms, including prophetic preaching and teaching, ministry initiatives, leadership in engaging spiritual disciplines, spiritual direction and mentoring. The critical issue of leadership is not who is in charge, but rather charging the Body of Christ with the imperatives of Christian discipleship. Professional ministers do not have to own the ideas or micromanage the process, but ministry entails spiritual leadership which is a legitimate expression of servanthood.

THE BIBLICAL CONCEPT OF COVENANT

The context of ministry is the covenant community, which is literally the people of God created and sustained in covenant. Covenant in scripture is a solemn promise which covenantal parties recognize as binding, and covenants which bind God and the people of God together pervade the Old Testament. In some covenants God binds Himself with a promise to the community (e.g., the covenant with Abraham in Gen. 12:1-3), and in others the community is bound by God's command (e.g., the Mosaic covenant in Exod. 20:1-17 and elsewhere). In every case there is a promise which one or both parties are bound to keep and which promise constitutes the covenant itself. So solemn is this promise that the prophets warn that the community's dereliction of the covenant will result in certain destruction.

In the New Testament covenantal language is consummated in the Christ event. In Jesus' life, death, and resurrection, God calls into being the people of the new covenant, symbolically enacted at the Last Supper in the sharing of the bread and the cup.

> **1 Corinthians 11:23-26** (NKJV) [23] For I received from the Lord that which I also delivered to you: that the Lord Jesus on the *same* night in which He was betrayed took bread; [24] and when He had given thanks, He broke *it* and said, "Take, eat; this is My body which is broken for you; do this in remembrance of Me." [25] In the same manner *He* also *took* the cup after supper, saying, "This cup is the new covenant in My blood. This do, as often as you drink *it,* in remembrance of Me." [26] For as often as you eat this bread and drink this cup, you proclaim the Lord's death till He comes.

The new covenant in Christ's blood realized the deepest sense and richest end of the covenants between God and Israel – the joyous surrender of the community to the One who calls the community to life through covenant love and indwelling Spirit. The power of covenant love is anticipated in the gospels ("The glory that you have given me I have given them, so that they may be one, I in them and You in Me, that they may become completely one")[i] and consummated at Pentecost ("All of them were filled with the Holy Spirit and began to speak in other languages, as the Spirit gave them ability").[ii] According to Acts, the Spirit-inspired unity which overcame language barriers led to the sharing of possessions:

> **Acts 2:44-47** (NKJV) [44] Now all who believed were together, and had all things in common, [45] and sold their possessions and goods, and divided them among all, as anyone had need. [46] So continuing daily with one accord in the temple, and breaking bread from house to house, they ate their food with gladness and simplicity of heart, [47] praising God and having favor with all the people. And the Lord added to the church daily those who were being saved.

Whatever else this and other descriptions[iii] of the early church may imply for contemporary practice, they unequivocally declare that God calls the church to be a covenant community in the Holy Spirit marked by a profoundly deep and cooperative fellowship:

> **Ephesians 4:1-6** (NKJV) [1] I, therefore, the prisoner of the Lord, beseech you to walk worthy of the calling with which you were called, [2] with all lowliness and gentleness, with longsuffering, bearing with one another in love, [3] endeavoring to keep the unity of the Spirit in the bond of peace. [4] *There is* one body and one Spirit, just as you were called in one hope of your calling; [5] one Lord, one faith, one baptism; [6] one God and Father of all, who *is* above all, and through all, and in you all.

That God's covenant community in the context for ministry shapes our understanding of ministry and ministerial ethics in several ways.

1. First, ministry is rightly described by plural rather than singular modifiers; ministry is ours, not mine. While we ordain some to vocational or professional ministry, we expect the whole covenant community to participate in ministry, and we honor the contributions of every member.

2. Second, ministry presupposes trusting relationships. In the face of the many things that tend to fracture the fellowship, the New Testament calls us to trust in and live by the unity which is ours in Christ.

3. Third, ministry is framed by the promise of mutual commitment and accountability. We are covenant-bound to support each other in building up the Body of Christ and to expect faithfulness and competence in ministry.

4. Fourth, ministry envisions individual and corporate initiatives held together in creative tension. We covenant neither to always wait for someone else to act on ministry opportunities nor to always assume that no one else is able and willing to act.

5. Fifth, we function as a community. We are not autonomous individuals who happen to come together on certain occasions because we hold similar interest. We are Christ's Body called to bear witness in our communal life that the Word became flesh and lives among us. The way we minister or fail to minister to one another and to the world in large measure corroborates or undermines our communal witness.

6. Sixth, we subordinate personal agendas to building up the whole Body. In fact, our willingness to work selflessly for the good of the community authenticates our covenant to live as a community. Among other things, this means we resist every move to splinter the community into competing special interests. We covenant to talk with each other and not about each other in the interest of common ministry.

THE CALL TO MINISTRY

To Abram: "*Go from your country and your kindred and your father's house to the land that I will show you*" (Gen. 12:1). To Moses: "*So come, I will send you to Pharaoh to bring my people, the Israelites*" (Exod. 3:10). To Isaiah: "*Whom shall I send, and who will go for us? . . . Go and say to this people*" (Isa. 6:8-9). To the Twelve: "*Follow me*" (Matt. 4:19).

These biblical texts exemplify the call of God on people's lives. Some people experience the call of God as a moment as powerful and dynamic as Moses before the burning bush (Exodus 3) or Saul blinded by the heavenly light (Acts 9). Others experience a call to a specific work or place of ministry like Deborah (Judges 4) or Mary (Luke 1). What is the call of God? Is it not the longings, yearnings, and desires that God places within the people of God to awaken them to and engage them in God's will, presence, and activity in the world? God uses a variety of avenues to call people, but common to each is God's sovereign choice, grace, and purpose for the good of humanity and the glory of God's Kingdom. God's call should elicit the faithful response of the person called and a way of life that honors the One who calls.

In calling us to the ministry of reconciliation (2 Cor. 5:18-19), God calls some to proclaim the gospel of reconciliation (Romans 10:14-15) and to equip others for Christian service and the building up of the church (Eph. 4:11-12). With the call of God comes the call to live in a manner worthy of the calling (Eph. 1:1). Unfortunately, not all of those called have lived up to the high ethical standards to the One who calls them and the Spirit who leads them. Paul lays the foundation and challenge of ethical behavior for those called as servant and vocational ministers:

> **1 Corinthians 4:1-2** (NKJV) [1] *Let a man so consider us, as servants of Christ and stewards of the mysteries of God.* [2] *Moreover it is required in stewards that one be found faithful.*

In Ephesians 5:1-5, Christians are admonished to imitate God, to live in love, and not to allow immorality, greed, and vulgarity in their lives. In Colossians 3:1-17, Paul counsels the church *"to set your minds on things that are above . . . put to death . . . whatever in you that is earthly . . . clothe yourselves with love, which binds everything together in perfect harmony."* Here and elsewhere in the New Testament, perfection is not a prerequisite for doing ministry, but ministers must be alert to the dangers that lead to moral and professional destruction.

Clearly, ministers should hear and heed the voice of God in their lives. God's call is not a one-time call, but one that requires the ongoing diligence of faithfulness to continue in obedience. Many leaders whose stories are told in scripture heard the voice of God initially only to be led astray by lesser voices in later life. For David, there was the temptation of sex; for Solomon, the idolatries of 700 wives and the undisciplined pursuit of pleasure; for Hezekiah, the pride of accumulated wealth; and for Josiah, the failure to discern the true voice of God even after years of blessing and walking with the Lord. Ministers must re-examine and renew the commitment to God's call over time.

First and foremost, this commitment is to be a follower of Jesus. The lifestyle, priorities, and morality of the called should reflect the image of Christ. The call to ministry is a call to faithfulness above and beyond any considerations regarding the size or temporal measure of the ministry to which ministers are called.

Ministers do well to remember not only the time and circumstances of their unique call, but the holiness and the character of the One who calls them. Because the minister's call is not just vocational, but intensely personal, ministerial accountability is intensely personal, and not based merely on outward performance. In remembering the call and the One who calls, ministers find nourishment for persevering through difficult times.

To sustain the call, ministers must work at maintaining their physical, mental, emotional, spiritual and moral well-being. The pressures of life and work can erode the sense of purpose with which ministry began. Ministers find sustaining strength to continue when other voices would bid them to abandon their ministries as they remember the God who calls and the work to which they have dedicated themselves. Faithful remembrance brings a profound sense of humility and joy.

FOR THE MINISTER:
- I will remember the holiness of the One who called me into ministry and seek to be conformed to the image of Christ in the power of the Holy Spirit.

- I will respond to the call of Christ with faithful obedience and count it a joyful privilege to be asked to serve in ministry.

- I will review and renew my sense of calling with humility

  born of God's grace and seek the wisdom of my church and other mentors in diligently fulfilling my role in God's kingdom.

FOR THE CHURCH:

- We will honor and respect the call of God in the lives of our ministers and count their service among us as a gift from God.

- We will seek to help our ministers fulfill God's call on their lives by being obedient to God's call on our own lives, affirming that our ministers are sent by God to equip and encourage us.

- Together with our ministers, we will serve Christ's church and Kingdom in answering the Lord's call on our lives until the final call comes.

CHAPTER 3
QUALIFIED LEADERSHIP

"An overseer, then, must be above reproach."

1 Timothy 3:2a

In a letter to a young presbyter named Nepotian dated A.D. 394, Jerome (A.D. 345-419) rebuked the churches of his day for their hypocrisy in showing more concern for the appearance of their church buildings than the careful selection of their church leaders: "Many build churches nowadays; their walls and pillars of glowing marble, their ceilings glittering with gold, their altars studded with jewels. Yet to the choice of Christ's ministers no heed is paid."[liii]

A similar error is repeated by multitudes of churches today. Many churches seem oblivious to the biblical requirements for their spiritual leaders as well as to the need for the congregation to properly examine all candidates for leadership in light of biblical standards (1 Tim. 3:10). This failure was dramatically highlighted when a leading evangelical journal in America brought together five divorced pastors and asked them to share their feelings, experiences, and views on divorce and the ministry. The journal's staff published the forum because they believed the growing problem of divorce among ministers needed to be faced openly and honestly. In fact, the article claimed that a recent survey of divorce rates in the United States showed that pastors had the third highest divorce rate – exceeded only by that of medical doctors and policemen![liv]

The pastors' thoughts on divorce were presented in the journal through an open forum format. Along with the forum, the journal published the responses of seven well-known evangelical leaders to the divorced pastors' comments. What is astounding about the article is that not one of the seven leaders mentioned the biblical

73

qualifications for leadership outlined in 1 Timothy or Titus! This article reveals a widespread ignorance within the Christian community concerning Scripture's vigorous insistence on God's qualifications for local church leaders. It also demonstrates that churches and denominations have substituted their own standards for the biblical ones.

THE NEED FOR QUALIFIED SHEPHERD ELDERS

The most common mistake made by churches that are eager to implement eldership is to appoint biblically unqualified men. Because there is always a need for more shepherds, it is tempting to allow unqualified, unprepared men to assume leadership in the church. This is, however, a time-proven formula for failure. A biblical eldership requires biblically qualified elders.

The overriding concern of the New Testament in relation to church leadership is for the right kind of men to serve as elders and deacons. The offices of God's Church are not honorary positions bestowed on individuals who have attended church faithfully or who are senior in years. Nor are they board positions to be filled by good friends, rich donors, or charismatic personalities. Nor are they positions that only graduate seminary students can fill. The church offices, both eldership and deaconship, are open to all who meet the apostolic, biblical requirements. The New Testament is unequivocally emphatic on this point:

- To the troubled church in Ephesus, Paul insists that a properly constituted Christian church (1 Tim. 3:14, 15) must have qualified, approved elders (1 Timothy 3:1-7).

- Paul also insists that prospective elders and deacons be publicly examined in light of the stated list of qualifications. He writes, "And let these [deacons] also [like the elders] first be tested [examined]; then let them serve as deacons if they are beyond reproach" (1 Timothy 3:10; 5:24-25).

74

- When directing Titus in how to organize churches on the island of Crete, Paul reminds Titus to appoint only morally and spiritually qualified men to be elders. By stating elder qualifications in a letter, Paul establishes a public list to guide the local church in its choice of elders and to empower it to hold its elders accountable (Titus 1:5-9).

- When writing to churches scattered throughout northwestern Asia Minor, Peter speaks of the kind of men who should be elders. He exhorts the elders to shepherd the flock "not under compulsion, but voluntarily, according to the will of God; and not for sordid gain, but with eagerness; nor yet as lording it over those allotted to your charge, but proving to be examples to the flock" (1 Peter 5:2-3).

It is highly noteworthy that the New Testament provides more instruction on the qualifications for eldership than on any other aspect of eldership. Such qualifications are not required for all teachers or evangelists. One may be gifted as an evangelist and be used of God in that capacity, yet be unqualified to be an elder. An individual may be an evangelist immediately after conversion, but Scripture says that a new convert cannot be an elder (1 Tim. 3:6). There are three critically important reasons why God demands these qualifications of church elders.

First, the Bible says that an elder must be of irreproachable moral character and capable in the use of Scripture because he is "God's steward," that is, God's household manager (Titus 1:7). An elder is entrusted with God's dearest and most costly possessions, His children. He thus holds a position of solemn authority and trust. He acts on behalf of God's interest. No earthly monarch would dare think of hiring an immoral or incapable person to manage his estate. Nor would parents think of entrusting their children or family finances to an untrustworthy or incompetent person. So, too, the High and Holy One will not have an unfit, unqualified steward caring for His precious children.

As stewards of God's household, elders have access to people's homes and the most intimate details of their lives. They have access to the people who are most vulnerable to deception or abuse. They also have the greatest influence over the doctrinal direction of the church. Therefore, church elders must be men who are well-known by the community, have proven integrity, and are doctrinally sound.

Second, local church elders are to be living examples for the people to follow (1 Peter 5:3). They are to model the character and conduct that God desires for all His children. Since God calls His people to "be blameless and innocent, children of God above reproach in the midst of a crooked and perverse generation" (Phil. 2:15), it is necessary that those who lead His people be morally above reproach and model godly living.

John MacArthur, well-known radio preacher and author, echoes this point when he writes: "Whatever the leaders are, the people become. As Hosea said, 'Like people, like priest' (4:9). Jesus said, 'Everyone, after he had been fully trained, will be like his teacher' (Luke 6:40). Biblical history demonstrates that people will seldom rise above the spiritual level of their leadership."[iv] Because people are like sheep, shepherd elders have an extraordinarily powerful impact on the behavior, attitudes, and thinking of the people:

- If the elders have a contentious spirit, the people will inevitably become contentious (1 Tim. 3:3; Titus 1:7).

- If the elders are inhospitable, the people will be unfriendly and cold (1 Tim. 3:2; Titus 1:8).

- If the elders love money, the people will become lovers of money (1 Tim. 3:3).

- If the elders are not sensible, balanced, and self-controlled, their judgment will be characterized by ugly extremes, which will cause the people to be extreme and unbalanced (1 Tim. 3:1-2; Titus 1:8).

- If the elders are not faithful, one-woman husbands, they will subtly encourage others to be unfaithful (1 Tim. 3:2; Titus 1:6).

- If the elders do not faithfully hold to the authority of the Word, the people will not hold to it (Titus 1:9).

Much of the weakness and waywardness of our churches today is due directly to our failure to require that ministers meet God's standards for office. If we want our local churches to be spiritually fit, then we must require our ministers to be spiritually fit.

Third, the biblical qualifications protect the church from incompetent or morally unfit leaders. Some people push themselves into positions of church leadership to satisfy their unholy egos. Others are sadly deceived about their own ability and character. And some are evildoers who are motivated by Satan to infiltrate and ruin churches. The public, objective, God-given qualifications for church leadership protect the congregation from such unfit people.

These observable, objective standards for elders are especially important when churches must deal with dominating, stubborn church leaders who are incapable of truly seeing their sins or heresies and yet must be discharged from office. The elder qualifications empower each congregation and its leaders with the right and the objective means to hold back or remove unfit men from leadership. To refuse to remove a sinful or doctrinally unsound elder, however, is willful disobedience to God's Word that will eventually undermine the moral and spiritual vitality of the whole church as well as the integrity of the leadership council. The refusal to remove an erring elder will also damage the church's credibility and gospel witness before an unbelieving community, which is a matter of utmost concern to Paul (1 Tim. 3:7). Thus the God-given standards for elders are essential for protecting the local church's spiritual welfare and evangelistic witness.

Today churches most need men of Christlike character to be in spiritual leadership. The best laws and constitutions are impotent without men who are "just," "devout," "sensible," "self-controlled," "forbearing," "uncontentious," "and faithful to sound doctrine. These are precisely the qualities that God requires of those who lead His people.

THE QUALIFICATIONS FOR SHEPHERD ELDERS

When we speak of the elder's qualifications, most people think these qualifications are something different from those of the clergy. The New Testament, however, has no separate standards for professional clergy and lay elders. The reason is simple. There are only two offices – elders and deacons. From the New Testament perspective, any man in the congregation who desires to shepherd the Lord's people and who meets God's requirements for the office can be a pastor elder.

As the lists show (1 Timothy 3:2-7; Titus 1:6-9; 1 Peter 5:1-3), God does not require wealth, social status, senior age, advanced academic degrees, or even great spiritual gifts of those who desire to shepherd His people. We do the congregation and the work of God a great disservice when we add our arbitrary requirements to God's qualifications. Man-made requirements inevitably exclude needed, qualified men from the pastoral leadership of the church.

To be faithful to Holy Scripture and God's plan for the local church, we must open the pastoral leadership of the church to all in the church who are called by the Holy Spirit (Acts 20:20) and meet the apostolic qualifications. Although such a plan may be abhorrent to the clerical mind-set, it represents an authentic, apostolic mind-set. According to the New Testament, the elders of the church are all the men of the local church who desire to lead the flock and are

78

scripturally qualified to do so. The Scriptural qualifications can be divided into three broad categories relating to moral and spiritual character, abilities, and Spirit-given motivation.

MORAL AND SPIRITUAL QUALIFICATIONS

Most of the biblical qualifications relate to the candidate's moral and spiritual qualities. The first and overarching qualification is that of being "above reproach." What is meant by "above reproach" is defined by the character qualities that follow the term. In both of Paul's lists of elder qualifications, the first specific character virtue itemized is, "the husband of one wife." That means that an elder must be above reproach in his marital and sexual life.

From the beginning, God sternly warned His people against the corrupt sexual practices of the heathen nations. He commanded His people to be holy and separate from the nations, to be faithful to the marriage covenant, and to be sexually pure. In the eighteenth chapter of Leviticus, Moses details all the sexual sins of the godless nations that would soon surround Israel. God warns His people against the practice of such sins: "Do not defile yourselves by any of these things [depraved sexual practices]; for by all these the nations which I am casting out before you have become defiled ... Thus you are to keep My charge, that you do not practice any of the abominable customs which have been practices before you, so as not to defile yourselves with them; I am the Lord your God" (Lev. 18:24, 30). The need for purity was taught to the new community as well. Paul writes, "But do not let immorality or any impurity or greed even be named among you, as is proper among saints" (Eph. 5:3).

One of Satan's oldest, most effective strategies for destroying the people of God is to adulterate the marriages of those who lead God's people (Num. 25:1-5; 1 Kings 11:1-13; Ezra 9:1-2). Satan knows that if he can defile the shepherd's marriage, the sheep will follow. The specific marital and family qualifications God requires for elders are meant to protect the whole church. So the church must insist that its leaders meet these qualifications before serving and while serving. If the local church does not insist on these requirements, the people will sink into the toxic wasteland of today's sexual and marital practices.

Tragically, many major Christian denominations have learned nothing from the Old Testament about the certain results of accommodating secular standards of sexual behavior. In nearly every major Christian denomination, God's laws regarding marriage, divorce, sexuality, and gender differences are being discarded and replaced with an acceptance of the most corrupt human practices. Among Christian leaders, adultery and other sexual sins are at epidemic levels. Among the major denominations, clergy divorce and remarriage is hardly an issue. As Time magazine aptly describes today's religious landscape, "Denominations that once would not tolerate divorced ministers now find themselves debating whether to accept avowed lesbian ones."[lvi]

The other character qualities stress the elders' integrity, self-control, and spiritual maturity. Since elders govern the church body, they must be self-controlled in the use of money, alcohol, and in the exercise of their pastoral authority. Since they are to be models of Christian living, they must be spiritually devout, righteous, lovers of good, hospitable, and morally above reproach before the non-Christian community. In pastoral work, relationship skills are preeminent. Thus shepherd elders must be gentle, stable, sound-minded, and uncontentious. Angry, hot-headed men hurt people. So an elder must not have a dictatorial spirit or be quick-tempered, pugnacious, or self-willed. Finally, an elder must not be a new Christian. He must be a spiritually mature, humble, time-proven disciple of Jesus Christ.

ABILITIES

In the catalogs of elder qualifications, three requirements address the elder's abilities to perform the task. He must be able to manage his household well, provide a model of Christian living for others to follow, and be able to teach and defend the faith.

Able to Manage the Family Household Well

An elder must be able to manage his household well. The Scripture states: "He must be one who manages his own household well, keeping his children under his control with all dignity (but if a man does not know how to manage his own household, how will he take care of the church of God?)" (1 Tim. 3:4-5). The Puritans referred to the family household as the "little church." This perspective is in keeping with the scriptural reasoning that if a man cannot shepherd his family, he can't shepherd the extended family of the church.

Managing the local church is more like managing a family than managing a business or state. A man may be a successful businessman, a capable public official, a brilliant office manager, or a top military leader but be a terrible church elder or father. Thus a man's ability to oversee his household well is a prerequisite for overseeing God's household.

What about single men or married men who have no children? Can these men be elders? Most definitely (1 Cor. 7:8-35)! The qualification regarding marriage and children should not be construed as commands to marry and have children. Rather, because most men are married and have children, the Scripture sets forth God's standard for church leaders who are husbands and fathers. Setting standards for married men who have children is quite a different issue from commanding marriage and fatherhood, which is not always a matter of choice. Single men and childless, married men can certainly be pastor elders. When they lack experience because of their unmarried or childless status, their fellow elders who are married and have children can fill in the gap. Single and childless men have a unique contribution to make to the flock and the eldership team. Of course the sexual conduct and home management of single and childless men must be above reproach, just as it must be above reproach for married men who have children.

Able to Provide a Model for Others to Follow

An elder must be an example of Christian living that others will want to follow. Peter reminds the Asian elders "to be examples to the flock" (1 Peter 5:3b). If a man is not a godly model for others to follow, he cannot be an elder, even if he is a good teacher and manager. Like Peter, Paul also recognized the importance of modeling Christ. He did his utmost to model Christ and expected the people to follow:

- Brethren, join in following my example, and observe those who walk according to the pattern you have in us (Phil. 3:17).

- Be imitators of me, just as I also am of Christ (1 Cor. 11:1).

- For you yourselves know how you ought to follow our example, because we did not act in an undisciplined manner among you ... but in order to offer ourselves as a model for you, that you might follow our example (2 Thess. 3:7, 9b).

- I exhort you, therefore, be imitators of me (1 Cor. 4:16; cf. Gal. 4:12; 1 Thess. 1:5-6; 1 Tim. 4:12; Titus 2:7).

The greatest way to inspire and influence people for God is through personal example. Character and deeds, not official position or title, is what really influences people for eternity. Today men and women crave authentic examples of true Christianity in action. Who can better provide the week-by-week, long-term examples of family life, business life, and church life than local church elders? This is why it is so important that elders, as living imitators of Christ, shepherd God's flock in God's way.

Able to Teach and Defend the Faith

An elder must be able to teach and defend the faith. It doesn't matter how successful a man is in his business, how eloquently he speaks, or how intelligent he is. If he isn't firmly committed to historic, apostolic doctrine and able to instruct people in biblical doctrine, he does not qualify as a biblical elder (Acts 20:28ff; 1 Tim. 3:2; Titus 1:9).

The New Testament requires that a pastor elder "[hold] fast the faithful word which is in accordance with the teaching" (Titus 1:9a). This means that an elder must firmly adhere to orthodox, historic, biblical teaching. Elders must not be chosen from among those who have been toying with new doctrines. Since the local church is "the pillar and support of the truth" (1 Tim. 3:15b), its leaders must be rock-solid pillars of biblical doctrine or the house will crumble. Since the local church is also a small flock traveling over treacherous terrain that is infested with "savage wolves," only those shepherds who know the way and see the wolves can lead the flock to its safe destination. An elder, then, must be characterized by doctrinal integrity.

It is essential for an elder to be firmly committed to apostolic, biblical doctrine so "that he may be able to exhort in sound doctrine and to refute those who contradict" (Titus 1:9b). This requires that a prospective elder has applied himself for some years to the reading and study of Scripture, that he can reason intelligently and logically discuss biblical issues, that he has formulated doctrinal beliefs, and that he had the verbal ability and willingness to teach others. There should be no confusion, then, about what a New Testament elder is called to do: he is to teach and exhort the congregation in sound doctrine and to defend the truth from false teachers. This is the big difference between board elders and pastor elders. New Testament elders are both guardians and teachers of sound doctrine.

For this reason, God's book, the Bible, is to be the prospective elder's continual course of study. The Bible is God's complete training manual for all spiritual leaders. Paul reminds Timothy that "from childhood you have known the sacred writings which are able to give you the wisdom that leads to salvation through faith in Christ Jesus" (2 Tim. 3:15). Paul further states that "all Scripture is inspired by God [God-breathed], and profitable for teaching, for reproof, correction, for training in righteousness; that the man of God may be adequate, equipped for every good work" (2 Tim. 3:16-17). Thus a man is unequipped for the shepherding task if he has not been schooled in God-breathed Holy Scripture. A shepherd who doesn't know the Bible is like a shepherd without legs; he can't lead or protect the flock.

How are prospective elders to be educated in God's book? First, if raised in godly, Christian homes, they will have had years of instruction in doctrine and holy living from the most effective teachers in the world, their mothers and fathers (Deut. 6:7; 11:19; Prov. 1:8; 4:1-5; Eph. 6:4; 1 Thess. 2:11; 1 Cor. 14:35; 2 Tim. 1:5; 3:15).[lvii]

Second, if the local church fulfills its role as a school for teaching apostolic doctrine, prospective elders will have been taught God's Word by gifted teachers. The Bible says that the local church is "the pillar and support of the truth" and "the household of God" (1 Tim. 3:15). This is why Paul charges Timothy to "give attention to the public reading of Scripture, to exhortation and teaching" (1 Tim. 4:13). Timothy was also to teach "faithful men, who will be able to teach others" (2 Tim. 2:2b). When Timothy departed from Ephesus, he expected that "faithful men," like the Ephesian elders, would teach future teachers and pastor elders who in turn would teach others.

Furthermore, the local church is not only a place to learn Scripture; it is the very best place to learn the skills required for shepherding people. It is in the local church that leaders learn to apply God's book to real-life situations. Thus the local church is to be God's school for the spiritual development of His children and the learning of Scripture (Acts 2:42; 11:26).

Third, a prospective elder learns the great truths of God through the consistent reading and study of Scripture and the ministry of the Holy Spirit (1 Cor. 2:12ff; 1 Thess. 4:9; 1 John 2:27). There is no substitute for a disciplined, persistent encounter with God through personal study of and meditation on Holy Scripture. In addition to studying Scripture, a growing Christian should be reading sound doctrinal material written by godly teachers of the Word.

Sadly, however, many churches (and Christian homes) have no vision for serious teaching or training in Scripture and doctrine. Other churches simply do not have the means to train their leaders; they are struggling to survive as a church body. Yet serious-minded believers hunger for in-depth teaching of the Scriptures. That is why Bible schools and seminaries will always be needed. Although there are problems with religious institutions that breed doubt in the authority of Scripture or reinterpret the Bible to agree with the spirit of the age, a good, Bible-believing and teaching school can provide excellent, in-depth training in Scripture.

I must warn, however, against the arbitrary requirement that many denominations impose on their shepherds to earn a master's degree before they are allowed to serve as a church pastor. God does not require advanced academic degrees as a qualification for spiritual leadership. When we set up formal academic standards, we professionalize the government of the church and create, at least in practice, a pastoral office that is separate from the eldership. We do not have God's authorization to establish such standards.

Do not forget that our Lord and Master, Jesus Christ, was not formally trained in a rabbinical school, although such training was available and very much prized in His day. Despite His lack of formal schooling in religion, however, Jesus was eminently educated in Scripture. Indeed, the people were so amazed by Jesus' knowledge and teaching as an untrained layman that they commented: "How has this man become learned, having never been educated?" (John 7:15b). The same observation was made of Jesus' close disciples: "as they observed the confidence of Peter and John, and understood that they were uneducated and untrained men, they were marveling, and began to recognize them as having been with Jesus" (Acts 4:13).

Unfortunately, many Christian people today are so clergy dependent that they can't imagine how men and women without formal theological training and the degrees that go with it can know the Bible and teach it effectively. We must remember that degrees are required in the world of business and academia, but they are not required to minister in the household of God. Some people who are not able to go to school are taught by Christ through the Holy Spirit. They are educated in His Word and thus, according to God's standards, are qualified to lead and teach His people.

Spirit-Given Motivation for the Task

An obvious but not insignificant qualification is the shepherd's personal desire to love and care for God's people. Paul and the first Christians applauded such willingness by creating a popular Christian saying: "If any man aspires to the office of overseer, it is a fine work he desires to do" (1 Tim. 3:1). Peter, too, insisted that an elder shepherd the flock willingly and voluntarily (1 Peter 5:2). He knew from years of personal experience that the shepherding task can't be done by someone that views spiritual care as an unwanted obligation. Elders who serve grudgingly or under constraint are incapable of genuine care for people. They will be unhappy, impatient, guilty, fearful, and ineffective shepherds. Shepherding God's people through this sin-weary world is far too difficult a task – fraught with too many problems, dangers, and demands – to be entrusted to someone who lacks the will and desire to do the work.

A true desire to lead the family of God is always a Spirit-generated desire. Paul reminded the Ephesian elders that it was the Holy Spirit – not the church or the apostles – who placed them as overseers in the church to shepherd the flock of God (Acts 20:28). It was the Spirit who called them to shepherd the church and who moved them to care for the flock. The Spirit planted the pastoral desire in their hearts. He gave the compulsion and strength to do the work and the wisdom and appropriate gifts to care for the flock. The elders were His wise choice for the task. In the church of God, it is not man's will that matters but God's will and arrangement. So the only men who qualify for eldership are those whom the Holy Spirit gives the motivation and gifts for the task.

A biblical eldership, then, is a biblically qualified team of shepherd leaders. A plurality of unqualified elders is of no benefit to the local church. It is better to have no elders than the wrong ones. The local church must in all earnestness insist on biblically qualified elders, even if such men take years to develop.

QUALIFICATIONS FOR MINISTERS (DEFINING THE WORDS)

1 Timothy 3:2-7	Titus 1:6-9	1 Peter 5:1-3
Above reproach	Above reproach	Not under compulsion, but voluntary
The husband of one wife	The husband of one wife	Not for sordid gain, but with eagerness
Temperate	Having children who believe	Not yet as lording it over … but proving to be examples
Prudent	Not self-willed	
Respectful	Not quick-tempered	
Hospitable	Not addicted to wine	
Able to teach	Not pugnacious	
Not addicted to wine	Not fond of sordid gain	
Not pugnacious	Hospitable	
Gentle	Lover of what is good	
Uncontentious	Sensible	
Free from the love of money	Just	
Manages his household well	Devout	
Not a new convert	Self-controlled	
A good reputation with those outside the Church	Holds fast the faithful Word both to exhort and to refute	

The character and effectiveness of any church is directly related to the quality of its leadership. That's why the Bible stresses the importance of qualified church leadership and delineates specific standards for evaluating those who would serve in that sacred position. Failure to adhere to those standards has caused many of the problems that churches throughout the world currently face.

It is significant that in his description of the qualifications for elders, Paul focused on their character rather than their function. A man is qualified because of what he is, not because of what he does. If he sins and thereby soils his character, he is subject to discipline in front of the entire congregation (1 Tim. 5:20). The church must carefully guard that sacred office.

The spiritual qualifications for leadership are nonnegotiable. They are part of what determines whether a man is indeed called by God to the ministry. Bible schools and seminaries can help equip a man for ministry, church boards and pulpit committees can extend opportunities for him to serve, but only God can call a man and make him fit for the ministry. The call to the ministry is not a matter of analyzing one's talents and then selecting the best career option. It's a Spirit-generated compulsion to be a man of God and serve Him in the church. Those whom God calls will meet the qualifications.

Why are the standards so high? Because whatever the leaders are, the people become. Hosea said, "Like people, like priest" (4:9). Jesus said, "Everyone, after he has been fully trained, will be like his teacher" (Luke 6:40). Biblical history demonstrates that people will seldom rise above the spiritual level of their leadership.

First Timothy 3 carefully outlines the spiritual qualifications for men in leadership. Paul is speaking specifically of elders' qualifications in the verses we will examine (vv. 1-7), but note that the only significant difference between an elder's qualifications and those of a deacon is that an elder must be skilled as a teacher (cf. vv. 1-7 and 8-13).

Paul begins by asserting that the man who desires the office desires a good work (v. 1). But no one should ever be placed into church leadership based on desire alone. It is the responsibility of the church to affirm a man's qualifications for ministry by measuring him against God's standard for leadership as delineated in verses 2-7.

"BLAMELESS" – HE IS A MAN OF UNQUESTIONABLE CHARACTER

Paul began, "a bishop [or elder] . . . must be blameless" (v. 2). The Greek word translated "must", emphasizes an absolute necessity: blamelessness is mandatory for overseers. It is a fundamental, universal requirement. In fact, the other qualifications listed by Paul in verses 2-7 define and illustrate what he meant by "blameless."

The Greek text indicates this is referring to a present state of blamelessness. It doesn't refer to sins that the man committed before he matured as a Christian – unless such sins remain as a blight on his life. (No one is blameless in that sense.) The idea is that he has sustained a reputation for blamelessness.

"Blameless" (v. 2) means "not able to be held." A blameless man cannot be taken hold of as if he were a criminal in need of detention for his actions. There's nothing to accuse him of. He is irreproachable. When an elder is irreproachable, critics cannot discredit his Christian profession of faith or prove him unfit to lead others (Neh. 6:13). He has a clean moral and spiritual reputation. Since all God's people are called to live holy and blameless lives (Phil. 2:15; 1 Thess. 5:23), since the world casts a critical eye at the Christian community (1 Peter 3:15, 16), and since Christian leaders lead primarily by their example (1 Peter 5:3), an irreproachable life is indispensable to the Christian leader. Job, for example, was an

90

elder among his people (Job 29:7, 21, 25; 31:21), and he, the Scripture says, was morally above reproach: "There was a man in the land of Uz, whose name was Job, and that man was blameless, upright, fearing God, and turning away from evil" (Job 1:1).

A church leader's life must not be marred by sin – be it an attitude, habit, or incident. That's not to say he must be perfect, but there must not be any obvious defect in his character. He must be a model of godliness so he can legitimately call his congregation to follow his example (Phil. 3:17). The people need to be confident that he won't lead them into sin.

Spiritual leaders must be blameless because they set the example for the congregation to follow. That is a high standard, but it isn't a double standard. Since you are responsible to follow the example of your godly leaders (Heb. 13:7, 17), God requires blamelessness of you as well. The difference is that certain sins can disqualify church leaders for life, whereas that's not necessarily true for less prominent roles in the church. Nevertheless, God requires blamelessness of all believers (cf. Eph. 1:4; 5:27; Phil. 1:10; 2:15; Col. 1:22; 2 Pet. 3:14; Jude 24). Paul now begins to delineate concrete, observable qualities that define what it means to be irreproachable.

"THE HUSBAND OF ONE WIFE" – HE IS SEXUALLY PURE

"The husband of one wife" is not the best rendering according to our studies of the Greek text. We believe the words translated "wife" (*gunaikos*) and "husband" (*aner*) are better translated "woman" and "man." The Greek construction places emphasis on the word *one*, thereby communicating the idea of a one-woman man.

It is appropriate that sexual fidelity is first on Paul's list of moral qualifications because that seems to be the area that most often disqualifies a man from ministry. It is therefore a matter of grave concern.

There have been many proposed interpretations of this qualification. The view that an elder can't have more than one wife at a time has been the traditional understanding of the English phrase "the husband of one wife," but although the religious climate of Paul's day did have some who engaged in this practice, we believe that there was a fuller meaning of the phrase.

Some people say that "the husband of one wife" means a man can't be an elder if he has remarried for any reason. But Paul couldn't have been referring to remarriage because he made clear that God permits remarriage after the death of one's spouse (1 Tim. 5:9-15; Rom. 7:2-3; 1 Cor. 7:39).

Others say that Paul was prohibiting divorced men from serving as elders. But if Paul were referring to divorce, he could have clarified the issue by saying. "An elder must be a man who has never been divorced." But even that statement would pose problems because the Bible teaches that remarriage after divorce is within God's will under three circumstances.

First, divorce is justified when one partner commits continuous sexual sin. Jesus said to the religious leaders, "It hath been said [by rabbinical tradition], Whosoever shall [divorce] his wife, let him give her a writing of divorcement" (Matt. 5:31). Many Jewish men were divorcing their wives for insignificant reasons, and the only requirement was to complete the necessary paperwork.

But Jesus said, "Whoever shall [divorce] his wife, except for the cause of fornication, causeth her to commit adultery [when she remarries]; and whosoever shall marry her that is divorced committeth adultery" (Matt. 5:32). That implies fornication is legitimate grounds for divorce.

We believe that the "fornication" mentioned in that context refers to extreme situations of unrelenting and unrepentant sexual sin. God graciously permits the innocent party to be free from the bondage to

92

such an evil partner. With that comes the freedom to remarry a believer.

Under Old Testament law, if a marriage partner committed adultery, he or she could be stoned to death. That would release the other partner from that marriage and free him or her to remarry. Although God no longer demands the death of an unfaithful spouse, the sin of adultery is no less serious. Should God's grace in sparing the life of the adulterer penalize the innocent party by demanding lifelong singleness? We don't think so. The grace that spares the adulterer's life also frees the innocent party to remarry.

Second, divorce is justified when an unbelieving partner leaves. In 1 Corinthians 7:15 Paul says, "If the unbelieving depart, let him depart. A brother or a sister is not under bondage in such cases; but God hath called us to peace." If an unbelieving partner wants out of the marriage, the believer is free to let him or her go. God doesn't require you to live in a state of war with such a partner.

Third, remarriage is permissible if the divorce and remarriage took place before either party was a Christian (1 Cor. 6:9-11). A caution should be added in this area. If an individual is brought up for a leadership position, then we must deal with potential drawbacks. A "proving time" would be necessary to determine the character qualities of the new marriage. All leaders must be willing to have their lives examined according to the specific areas mentioned as qualifications.

*** **For a full statement of Marriage, Divorce and Remarriage see Master Builder Ministries' position paper on the same.**

Some people say 1Timothy 3:2 prohibits single men from serving as elders. But that position is refuted by the fact that Paul, who was an elder (1 Tim. 4:14; 2 Tim. 1:6), was himself single (1 Cor. 7:7-9).

The phrase "one-woman man" doesn't refer to marital status at all.

Paul is giving moral qualifications for spiritual leadership, not outlining what an elder's social status or external condition is to be. "One-woman man" speaks of the man's character, the state of his heart. If he is married, he is to be devoted solely to his wife. Whether or not he is married, he is not to be a ladies' man.

Unfortunately, it is possible to be married to one woman, yet not be a one-woman man. Jesus said, "Whosoever looketh on a woman to lust after her hath committed adultery with her already in his heart" (Matt. 5:28). First Timothy 3:2 is saying that a married – or unmarried-man who lusts after women is unfit for ministry. An elder must love, desire, and think only of the wife that God has given him.

Sexual purity is a major issue in the ministry. That's why Paul placed it at the top of his list.

"TEMPERATE" – HE IS NOT GIVEN TO EXCESS

The Greek word translated "temperate (*nephalios*) means without wine or not mixed with wine. It speaks of sobriety – the opposite of intoxication. Wine was a common drink in biblical times. Because Palestine was so hot and dry, it was often necessary to consume a large volume of wine to replenish body fluids lost in the heat. To help avoid drunkenness, wine was normally mixed with large amounts of water. Even so, the lack of refrigeration and the fermentative properties of wine made intoxication a problem.

Even though wine could cheer a person's heart (Judg. 9:13) and was beneficial for medicinal purposes such as stomach ailments (1 Tim. 5:23) and relieving pain for those near death (Prov. 31:6), its abuse was common. That's why Proverbs 20:1 says, "Wine is a mocker, strong drink is raging, and whosoever is deceived thereby is not wise."

Proverbs 23:29-35 says, "Who hath woe? Who hath sorrow? Who hath contentions? Who hath babbling? Who hath wounds without cause? Who hath redness of eyes? They that tarry long at the wine; they that go to seek mixed wine look not thou upon the wine when it is red, when it giveth its color in the cup, when it moveth itself aright. At the last it biteth like a serpent, and it stingeth like an adder. Thine eyes shall behold strange things, and thine heart shall utter perverse things. Yea, thou shalt be as he that lieth down in the midst of the sea, or as he that lieth upon the top of a mast. They have stricken me, shalt thou say, and I was not sick; they have beaten me, and I felt it not. When shall I awake? I will seek it again?"

Genesis 9 records an example of the mocking effect of wine. Noah planted a vineyard, made wine, and became drunk. While he was drunk "he was uncovered within his tent" (v. 21). The Hebrew text implies some kind of sexual evil. Ham, one of his sons, saw him in that state and mocked him. His two other sons entered the tent backward to cover him up because they were ashamed of his sinfulness.

Because of their position, example, and influence, certain Jewish leaders abstained from wine. Priests could not enter God's house while under its influence (Lev. 10:9). Kings were also advised not to consume wine because it might hinder their judgment (Prov. 31:4-5). The Nazirite vow, the highest vow of spiritual commitment in the Old Testament, forbade its participants from drinking wine (Num. 6:3). In the same way, spiritual leaders today must avoid intoxication so they may exercise responsible judgment and set an example of Spirit-controlled behavior.

It's likely that Paul's usage of *nehalios* went beyond the literal sense of avoiding intoxication to the figurative sense of being alert and watchful. An elder must deny any excess in life that diminishes clear thinking and sound judgment. "Temperate" denotes self-control, balanced judgment, and freedom from debilitating excesses or rash behavior. Negatively, it indicates the absence of any personal disorder that would distort a person's judgment or conduct. Positively, it describes a person who is stable, circumspect, self-restrained, and clear-headed.

It is necessary that elders, who face many serious problems, pressures, and decisions, be mentally and emotionally stable. Elders who lack a balanced mental, and emotional perspective, can easily be snared by the devil or false teachers.

"SOBER-MINDED" – HE IS SELF-DISCIPLINED

The Greek word translated "sober-minded" (*Sophron*) speaks of discipline or self-control. It's the result of being temperate (v. 2). The temperate man avoids excess so that he can see things clearly, and the clarity of thought leads to an orderly, disciplined life. He knows how to order his priorities.

Sophron indicates a person who is serious about spiritual things. Such a man doesn't have the reputation of a clown. That doesn't mean he avoids humor – any good leader is able to use and enjoy humor. But he is to have an appreciation for what really matters in life.

Similar to the word "temperate," "prudent" (*sophron*) also stresses self-control, particularly as it relates to exercising good judgment, discretion, and common sense. To be prudent is to be sound-minded, discreet, and sensible, able to keep an objective perspective in the face of problems and disagreements. Prudence is an essential quality of mind for a person who must exercise a great deal of practical discretion in handling people and their problems. Prudence tempers pride, authoritarianism, and self-justification.

Dictionary definitions of prudent commonly include these elements: caution, practical wisdom, and carefulness, understanding the present. In Proverbs, a prudent man "covereth shame" and

96

"looketh well to his ways" and "responds to correction" and is "hungry for training." (Proverbs 12:16, 23; 13:16; 14:8, 15, 18; 15:5; 16:21; 18:15; 19:14; 22:3; 27:12).

"GOOD BEHAVIOR" – HE IS WELL-ORGANIZED (RESPECTABLE)

The Greek word translated "good behavior" is *kosmios*. It comes from the root word *kosmos*, which in its general sense refers to the interplay between human, divine, and satanic values. A man of "good behavior" approaches all the aspects of his life in a systematic, orderly manner. *Kosmios* conveys the ideas of self-control, proper behavior, and orderliness. Although the word is used to describe properness in outward demeanor and dress in 1 Timothy 2:9, its usage here conveys the more general meaning of "orderly" ... "well-behaved," or "virtuous" ... that which causes a person to be regarded as "respectable" by others. An elder cannot expect people to follow him if he is not respectable.

This kind of person diligently fulfills his many duties and responsibilities. His disciplined mind produces disciplined actions – "good behavior."

The opposite of *kosmios* is chaos. Elders must not have a chaotic lifestyle. That's because their work involves administration, oversight, scheduling, and establishing priorities.

The ministry is no place for a man whose life is a continual confusion of unaccomplished plans and unorganized activities. Over the years I have seen many men who had difficulty ministering effectively because they couldn't get their lives into meaningful order. They couldn't concentrate on a task or systematically set and accomplish goals. Such disorder is a disqualification.

Paul is saying here that a man who is respectable has a lifestyle that adorns the teachings of the Bible in his speech, his dress, his appearance at home, his office or the way he does business. God is a God of order. A man of God, too, should be orderly and proper (1 Thess. 4:10-12; Col. 3:23-24; 1 Tim. 6:2; Col. 4:5-6; 1 Pet. 2:12; Phil. 1:27).

"JUST" – HE IS RIGHTEOUS OR UPRIGHT

"Just" (*dikaios*) means "righteous" or "upright." To be righteous is to live in accordance with God's righteous standards, to be law-abiding. John writes that "the one who practices righteousness is righteous, just as He is righteous" (1 John 3:7).

An elder who is righteous can be counted on to be a principled man and to make fair, just, and righteous decisions for the church (Prov. 29:7). Job is a good example of a just man:

> **Job 1:1** There was a man in the land of Uz, whose name *was* Job; and that man was perfect and upright, and one that feared God, and eschewed evil.

> **Job 29:14-17** I put on righteousness, and it clothed me: my judgment *was* as a robe and a diadem. I was eyes to the blind, and feet *was* I to the lame. I *was* a father to the poor: and the cause *which* I knew not I searched out. And I brake the jaws of the wicked, and plucked the spoil out of his teeth.

God's steward, then, must be like Job. He must live a morally upright life and be clothed in practical righteousness.

"GIVEN TO HOSPITALITY" – HE IS HOSPITABLE

The Greek word translated "given to hospitality" is composed of the words *xenos* ("stranger") and *phileo* ("to love" or "show affection"). It means to love strangers.

It is necessary for an elder to be hospitable. Hospitality is a concrete expression of Christian love and family life. It is an important biblical virtue:

- Job, the exemplary Old Testament elder, was a model of hospitality: "The alien has not lodged outside, For I have opened my doors to the traveler" (Job 31:32).

- Paul exhorts the Christians at Rome to pursue hospitality (Rom. 12:13).

- Peter writes, "Be hospitable to one another without complaint" (1 Peter 4:9).

- The author of Hebrews bids his readers: "Do not neglect to show hospitality to strangers, for by this some have entertained angels without knowing it" (Heb. 13:2).

These New Testament commands to practice hospitality are all found within the larger context of Christian love. Unfortunately, most Christians, and even some Christian leaders, are unaware that hospitality is a biblical requirement for pastoral leadership in the church. Some may even argue against such a seemingly insignificant point being a requirement for church shepherds.

Such thinking, however, shows an inadequate understanding of authentic Christian community, agape love, and the elder's work. For an elder to be inhospitable is a poor example of Christian love and care for others. The shepherd elder is to give himself lovingly and sacrificially for the care of the flock. This cannot be done from a distance – with a smile and a handshake on Sunday morning or through a superficial visit. Giving oneself to the care of God's people means sharing one's life and home with others. An open home is a sign of an open heart and a loving, sacrificial, serving spirit. A lack of hospitality is a sure sign of selfish, lifeless, loveless Christianity.

Although the shepherd's ministry of hospitality may seem like a small thing, it has an enormous, lasting impact on people. If you doubt this, ask those to whom a shepherd has shown hospitality. Invariably they will say that it is one of the most important, pleasant, memorable aspects of the shepherd's ministry.

In His mysterious ways, God works through the guest-host relationship to encourage and instruct His people. So we must never underestimate the power of hospitality in ministering to people's needs. Those who love hospitality love people and are concerned about them. If the local church's elders are inhospitable, the local church will also be inhospitable and indifferent toward the needs of others.

Biblical hospitality is showing kindness to strangers, not friends. In Luke 14:12-14 Jesus says, "When you give a luncheon or a dinner, do not invite your friends or your brothers or your relatives or rich neighbors, lest they also invite you in return, and repayment comes to you. But when you give a reception, invite the poor, the crippled, the lame, the blind, and you will be blessed, since they do not have the means to repay you; for you will be repaid at the resurrection of the righteous" (NASB).

"LOVING WHAT IS GOOD" – HE LOVES PEOPLE

Closely associated with hospitality, "loving what is good" is a positive virtue that is required of those who seek to help others and live as Christ-like examples. The Greek word used here is *philagathos*, which one Greek lexicon defines as "one who willingly and *with self-denial* does good, or is kind." William Hendriksen explains the word as "ready to do what is beneficial to others." The *Theological Dictionary of the New Testament* states: "According to the interpretation of the early Church it relates to the unwearying activity of love."

King David was a lover of goodness. He spared his enemy Saul, who had to reluctantly admit: "And you have declared today that you have done good to me, that the Lord delivered me into your hand and yet you did not kill me. For if a man finds his enemy, will he let him go away safely?" (1 Sam. 24:18, 19a). David sought to show kindness to his deceased friend Jonathan, Saul's son, by taking Jonathan's crippled son, Mephibosheth, into his own house (2 Sam. 9).

Job's friends had to admit that he was a lover of goodness: "Behold, you have admonished many, And you have strengthened weak hands. Your words have helped the tottering to stand, And you have strengthened feeble knees" (Job 4:3, 4). But the greatest example of one who loved goodness is our Lord Jesus Christ, who "went about doing good" (Acts 10:38b).

An elder who loves goodness seeks to do helpful, kind things for people. He will be loving, generous, and kind toward all and will never sink to evil, retaliatory behavior (Acts 11:24; Rom. 12:21; 15:2; Gal. 6:10; 1 Thess. 5:15; 1 Peter 3:13). In contrast, Paul prophesied that in the last days more people would be "lovers of self, lovers of money ... without self-control ... haters of good." (2 Tim. 3:3). A society that is led by lovers of good rather than haters of good is truly blessed.

"APT TO TEACH" – HE IS SKILLED IN TEACHING

The Greek word translated "apt to teach" (*didaktikon*) is used only two times in the New Testament (here and in 2 Tim. 2:24). It means "skilled in teaching." It's the only qualification listed here that relates to the function of an elder and sets the elder apart from the deacon.

Like Israel, the Christian community is built on Holy Scripture. So those who oversee the community must be able to guide and protect it by instruction from Scripture. According to Acts 20, the elders must shepherd the flock of God. A major part of shepherding the flock involves feeding it the Word of God. Therefore, elders must be "able to teach" in order to do their job.

The ability to teach entails three basic elements: a knowledge of Scripture, the readiness to teach, and the ability to communicate. This doesn't mean that an elder must be an eloquent orator, a dynamic lecturer, or a highly gifted teacher (of which there are very few). But an elder must know the Bible and be able to instruct others from it.

In his parallel list of elder qualifications in Titus, Paul expands on the meaning of "able to teach." He writes, "holding fast the faithful word which is in accordance with the teaching, that he [the elder] may be able both to exhort in sound doctrine and to refute those who contradict" (Titus 1:9). An elder, then, must be able to open his Bible and exhort and encourage others from it. He must also be able to discern false doctrine and refute it with Scripture. God's Word brings growth to the church and protects it from falsehood. Therefore, shepherd elders must be able to teach God's Word.

The Holy Spirit gives the gift of teaching to those called to teach the church (Rom. 12:7; 1Cor. 12:28; Eph. 4:11). It is not a natural ability but a Spirit-given endowment that enables one to teach the Word of God effectively.

"NOT GIVEN TO WINE" – HE IS NOT A DRINKER

The Greek word translated "given to wine" (*paroinos*) means "one who drinks." It doesn't refer to a drunkard – that's an obvious disqualification. The issue here is the man's reputation: Is he known as a drinker?

The Bible contains many warning against the potential dangers of wine and strong drink (Isa. 5:11, 22; Prov. 20:1; 23:30-35; Hos. 4:11). It especially warns leaders about the dangers of alcohol (Prov. 31:4, 5; Lev. 10:8-9; Isa. 28:1, 7, 8; 56:9-12).

Elders work with people, often those who are troubled. If an elder has a drinking problem, he will lead people astray and bring reproach upon the church. His overindulgence will interfere with spiritual growth and service, and it may well lead to more degrading sins.

While Paul is talking about over-drinking, the kind of drinking that causes one to lose control of his senses and be brought into bondage, a higher law rules us in this matter. We should not do "anything by which your brother stumbles" (Rom. 14:21).

"NOT VIOLENT" – HE IS NOT A FIGHTER

You can't be an elder if you settle disputes with your fists or in other violent ways. The Greek word translated "violent" (*plektes*) means "a giver of blows" or "a striker." An elder isn't quick-tempered and doesn't resort to unnecessary physical violence. That qualification is closely related to "not given to wine" because such violence is usually connected with people who drink excessively.

A pugnacious man carries a chip on his shoulder and is always ready for a good argument, perhaps even just a good theological tussle! A pugnacious person loses control of his senses and is controlled by anger. He is always ready to fight with a combative, belligerent nature. He cannot always avoid engaging in physical violence.

Elders must handle highly emotional interpersonal conflicts and deeply felt doctrinal disagreements between believers. Elders are often at the center of very tense situations, so a bad-tempered, pugnacious person is not going to solve issues and problems. He will, in fact, create worse explosions. Because a pugnacious man will treat the sheep roughly and even hurt them, he cannot be one of Christ's under-shepherds.

A spiritual leader must be able to handle things with a cool mind and a gentle spirit. Paul said, "The servant of the Lord must not strive" (2 Tim. 2:24).

"PATIENT" – HE EASILY PARDONS HUMAN FAILURE

We skipped "not greedy of filthy lucre," which appears in the King James Version but not in the better Greek manuscripts. That qualification is identical in meaning to "not covetous" (v. 3), which we will soon cover.

The Greek word translated "patient" (*epieikes*) means "to be considerate, genial, forbearing, gracious, or gentle." "Gentle" is one of the most attractive and needed virtues required of an elder. No English word adequately conveys the fullness of this word's beauty and richness. "Forbearing," "kind," "gentle," "magnanimous," "equitable," and "gracious" all help capture the full range of its meaning. Forbearance comes from God and is a chief source of peace and healing among His people. So in his letter to the Philippian Christians, who were experiencing internal as well as external conflict, Paul says, "Let your forbearing spirit be known to all men" (Phil. 4:5).

The gentle man stands in vivid contrast to the pugnacious man. A gentle man exhibits a willingness to yield and patiently makes allowances for the weakness and ignorance of the fallen human condition. One who is gentle refuses to retaliate in kind for wrongs done by others and does not insist upon the letter of the law or his personal rights. "Graciously amenable," says one commentator, "yielding wherever yielding is possible rather than standing up for one's rights."

104

Forbearance is a characteristic of God: "For Thou, Lord, art good, and ready to forgive [the same Greek word used in the LXX meaning forbearing or gentle], and abundance in loving-kindness to all who call upon Thee" (Ps. 86:5). Gentleness also characterized the life of Jesus on earth: "Now I Paul myself urge you by the meekness and gentleness of Christ" (2 Cor.10:1). God fully expects His under-shepherds to shepherd His people in the same way He does. He will not let His people be driven, beaten, condemned, or divided. Thus the shepherd must be patient, gracious, and understanding with the erring – and at times, exasperating – sheep. So many wrongs, disagreements, faults, hurts, and injustices exist in this sinful world that one would be forced to live in perpetual division, anger, and conflict were it not for forbearance. So elders must be "gentle" and "forbearing" like Christ.

In a practical sense, patience is the ability to remember good and forget evil. You don't keep a record of wrongs people committed against you (cf. 1 Cor. 13:5). That's an important virtue for a spiritual leader.

"NOT SELF-WILLED" – HE IS NOT ARROGANT

To be self-willed or arrogant is the opposite of being "gentle" [forbearing], which is one of the qualifications listed in 1 Timothy 3:3. A self-willed man wants his own way. He is stubborn, arrogant, and inconsiderate of others' opinions, feelings, or desires. A self-willed man is headstrong, independent, self-assertive, and ungracious, particularly toward those who have a different opinion. A self-willed man is not a team player, and the ability to work as a team is essential to eldership.

We must remember that the local congregation belongs to God, not to the overseer. The overseer is God's servant, not a master or owner, thus he has no right to be self-willed when caring for God's precious people. A self-willed man will scatter God's sheep because he is unyielding, overbearing, and blind to the feelings and opinions of others (2 Peter 2:10).

"NOT A BRAWLER" – HE IS NOT QUARRELSOME

The Greek word translated "not a brawler" (*amachos*) is similar in meaning to *me plektes* ("not violent," v. 3). The difference is that the latter refers to not being physically violent, whereas the former refers to not being quarrelsome. This signifies someone who is not quarrelsome and contentious, but is peaceable, a man of peace.

The contentious person domineers others, but in reality is insecure and defensive. He struggles against others, has to compete and debate others. He is not happy unless he is in charge and not willing to serve or come under anyone else. He is not willing to bend, not flexible. "It's my way or no way!" Such people, usually jealous and selfish, are motivated by pride. He is apt to contend and argue and loves controversy, strife, conflict, struggle and discord.

God hates division and fighting among His people: "These are six things which the Lord hates ... A false witness who utters lies, and one who spreads strife among brothers" (Prov. 6:16-19). Yet fighting paralyzes and kills many local churches. It may be the single, most distressing problem Christian leaders face. Therefore, a Christian elder is required to be "uncontentious," which means "not fighting" or "not quarrelsome."

By contrast, the peaceable character quality that makes a person a good elder is that he seeks peace. "With all that lies within you . . . live at peace with one another" is his motto (Romans 12:16, 18).

When you have a plurality of church leaders attempting to make decisions, you can't get very far if any of them are quarrelsome. That's why Paul said, "The servant of the Lord must not strive, but be gentle unto all men . . . patient" (2 Tim. 2:24). He must be a peacemaker.

"NOT QUICK-TEMPERED: HE IS SLOW TO ANGER"

One of God's attributes is that He is slow to anger, so His stewards must also be slow to anger. Man's anger is a hindrance to the work of God, "for the anger of a man does not achieve the righteousness of God" (James 1:20). Since an elder must deal with the people and their problems, a "hothead" will quickly find much material to fuel his anger. Proverbs warns against the perils of an angry man: "An angry man stirs up strife, And a hot-tempered man abounds in transgression" (Prov. 29:22). With his ugly, angry words, a quick-tempered man will destroy the peace and unity of God's family. The fierce looks and harsh words of the quick-tempered man will tear people apart emotionally, leaving people sick and destroyed in spirit. So a man who desires to be a church shepherd must be patient and self-controlled.

Of course, everyone experiences anger, and leaders who must deal with contentious situations often may experience a great deal of anger.

"NOT COVETOUS" – HE IS FREE FROM THE LOVE OF MONEY

The Greek word translated "not covetous" (*aphilarguros*) is a negation of the Greek words for "love" and "silver." It speaks of someone who doesn't love money. An elder must not love money or be greedy. So this qualification prohibits a base, mercenary interest that uses Christian ministry and people for personal profit. Both Paul and Peter condemn what we would call "being in it for the money" (1 Peter 5:2; Titus 1:7). False teachers, Paul points out, are overly interested in money and in personal financial gain (1 Tim. 6:5; Titus 1:11). The Pharisees were lovers of money who devoured widows' houses (Luke 16:14; Mark 12:40). The chief religious leaders of Jesus' day turned the temple into a merchandise mart for their own profit (Mark 11:15-17).

An elder should be content with God's provision. In Hebrews 13:5 the writer exhorts his readers, "Let your character be free from the love of money, being content with what you have; for He Himself has said, 'I will never desert you, nor will I ever forsake you.'" Paul states the matter this way: "For we have brought nothing into the world, so we cannot take anything out of it either. And if we have food and covering, with these we shall be content. But those who want to get rich fall into temptation and a snare and many foolish and harmful desires which plunge men into ruin and destruction" (1 Tim. 6:7-9). Elders, then, must model godly contentment and faith in Christ's loving provision for them.

"ONE THAT RULES WELL" – HE MAINTAINS A GODLY FAMILY

First Timothy 3:3-4 says that an overseer must be "one that rules well his own house, having his children in subjection with all gravity. (For if a man knows not how to rule his own house, how shall he take care of the church of God?)." An elder's home life is an essential consideration. Before he can lead in the church he must demonstrate his spiritual leadership within the context of his family.

The Greek word translated "rules" means "to preside, having authority over, stand before, or manage." He is the manager of his home. That affirms the consistent biblical teaching on male headship in the home. Obviously there are shared responsibilities between husband and wife and many tasks that the wife manages within the home, but the husband must be the leader.

The same Greek word is used in 1 Timothy 5:17: "Let the elders that rule well be counted worthy of double honor." An elder's ability to rule the church is affirmed in his home. Therefore he must be a

108

strong spiritual leader in the home before he is qualified to lead in the church.

He must rule his home "well." There are many men, who rule their home, but they don't rule very well – they don't get the desired results.

By implication a man's home includes his resources. A man may love the Lord and be spiritually and morally qualified to be an elder. He may even be skilled in teaching and have a believing wife and children who follow his leadership in the home, but let's say he has mismanaged his funds and is in bankruptcy. Somehow he can't seem to pull his finances into proper order. Since in the area of finances he doesn't rule his household well, he is disqualified from spiritual leadership. Stewardship of possessions is a critical test of a man's leadership. His home is a proving ground where his administrative capabilities can be clearly demonstrated.

The Greek word translated "subjection" is a military term that speaks of lining up in rank under those in authority. His children are to be lined up under his authority: respectful, controlled, and disciplined. That qualification applies only if a man has children. He's not disqualified if he doesn't have children. But if God has given him children, they must be under control and respectful to their parents.

A well-managed family means that children obey and submit to the father's leadership. The way in which that relationship is manifested is especially important: it is to be "with all dignity." The father is not to be a spirit-crushing tyrant who gains submission by harsh punishment. Elsewhere Paul writes, "Fathers, do not provoke your children to anger; but bring them up in the discipline and instruction of the Lord" (Eph. 6:4). Thus a Christian father must control his children in an honorable, respectful, and dignified way. Of course there are no perfect, problem-free children in this world. Even the best Christian fathers and mothers have child-rearing problems, but these parents resolve the problems and are involved with their children in responsible, caring ways. They guide their children through the many storms of life.

The translation, "having children who believe," found in Titus 1:5-6, is better rendered as "having faithful children," which is the choice in the *Authorized King James Version*. The Greek word for "believe" is *pistos*, which can be translated either actively as "believing" (1 Tim. 6:2) or passively as "faithful," "trustworthy," or "dutiful" (2 Tim. 2:2).

The contrast made is not between believing and unbelieving children, but between obedient, respectful children and lawless, uncontrolled children. The strong terms "dissipation or rebellion" stress the children's behavior, not their eternal state. A faithful child is obedient and submissive to the father. The concept is similar to that of the "faithful servant" who is considered to be faithful because he or she obeys the Master and does what the Master says (Matt. 24:45-51).

The parallel passage in 1 Timothy 3:4 states that the prospective elder must keep "his children under control with all dignity." Since 1 Timothy 3:4 is the clearer passage, it should be allowed to help interpret the ambiguity of Titus 1:6. "Under control with all dignity" is closely parallel with "having trustworthy children." In the Titus passage, however, the qualification is stated in a positive form – the elder must have children who are trustworthy and dutiful.

Those who interpret this qualification to mean that an elder must have believing, Christian children place an impossible burden upon a father. Even the best Christian fathers cannot guarantee that their children will believe. Salvation is a supernatural act of God. God, not good parents (although they are certainly used of God), ultimately brings salvation (John 1:12, 13).

In striking contrast to faithful children are those who are wild or insubordinate: "not accused of dissipation or rebellion." These are very strong words. "Dissipation" means "debauchery," "profligacy," or "wild, disorderly living" (1 Peter 4:3, 4; Luke 15:13). "Rebellion" means to be "disobedient," "unruly," or "insubordinate." Wild, insubordinate children are a terrible reflection on the home, particularly on the father's ability to guide and care for others. A man who aspires to eldership but has profligate children is not a viable candidate for church leadership.

"NOT A NOVICE" – HE IS A MATURE CHRISTIAN

Scripture prohibits a "new convert" from serving as an elder. A new convert is a beginner in the faith, a baby Christian, a recent convert. No matter how spiritual, zealous, knowledgeable, or talented a new convert may be, he is not spiritually mature. Maturity requires time and experience for which there is no substitute, so a new convert is simply not ready for the arduous task of shepherding God's flock.

There is nothing wrong with being "a new convert." All Christians begin life in Christ as babies and grow to maturity. An elder, however, must be mature and know his own heart. A new Christian does not know his own heart or understand the craftiness of the enemy, so he is vulnerable to pride – the most subtle of all temptations and most destructive of all sins. Pride caused the devil's ruin (Ezek. 28:11-19; Gen. 3:5, 14, 15). Like the devil, the prideful elder will inevitably fall. "Pride goes before destruction," the Bible says, "And a haughty spirit before stumbling" (Prov. 16:18; 11:2; 18:1; 29:23). Biblical history shows that pride has destroyed the greatest of men (2 Chron. 26:16; 32:25).

The position of elder (especially in a large, well-established church such as the one in Ephesus) carries considerable honor and authority. For a recent convert, the temptation of pride would be too great. Pride would destroy the man, causing personal disgrace, loss, exposure, divine chastisement, and possibly wrecking his faith. It would also hurt the church. So Paul warns against appointing a new convert as an elder, "lest he become conceited and fall into the condemnation incurred by the devil."

"A GOOD REPORT OF THEM WHO ARE OUTSIDE" – *HE IS WELL-RESPECTED BY NON-CHRISTIANS*

Finally, and of significant importance, an elder "must have a good reputation with those outside the church." Both the apostles Paul and Peter expressed deep concern that Christians have a good reputation before a watching, non-believing world (1 Cor. 10:32; Phil. 2:15; Col. 4:5-6; 1 Thess. 4:11-12; 1 Tim. 2:1-2; 5:14; 6:1; Titus 2:5, 8, 10; 3:1-2; 1 Peter 2:12, 15; 3:1, 16). If all believers are required to have a good testimony before non-Christians, then it is imperative that the leaders have a good reputation with unbelievers. The church's evangelistic credibility and witness is tied to the moral reputation of its leaders.

In reality, the non-Christians may know more about the character and conduct of the prospective elder than the church. Quite often the prospective elder's non-Christian fellow workers or relatives actually have more daily contact with the church leader than do the people in church. So Paul is concerned that those who may judge less sympathetically, but perhaps also more realistically and knowledgeably, will render a good verdict both from the perspective of their own consciences and also from their awareness of the particular man's commitment and consistency in terms of his Christian faith.

An outsider's opinion of a Christian leader's character cannot be dismissed, for it affects the evangelistic witness of the entire church, "the pillar and support of the truth." That is why Paul emphatically states "he must have a good reputation." The verb "must," the same verb used in verse 2, again stresses the absolute necessity and importance of this matter.

The reason for emphatically insisting on this qualification is that an elder with an unfavorable or sinful reputation among non-Christians will "fall into reproach and the snare of the devil" in a far more destructive way than those he leads. If a pastor elder has a reputation among non-believers as a dishonest businessman, a womanizer, or adulterer, the unbelieving community will take special note of his hypocrisy. Non-Christians will say, "He acts that way, and he's a church elder!" They will ridicule and mock him. They will scoff at the people of God. They will talk about him and will generate plenty of sinister gossip. They will raise tough, embarrassing questions. He will be discredited as a Christian leader and suffer disgrace and insults. His influence for good will be ruined, and he will endanger the church's evangelistic mission. The elder will certainly become a liability to the church, not a spiritual asset.

But that is not all. Fully aware of the devil's ways (2 Cor. 2:11), Paul adds that the defamed elder will also fall into "the snare of the devil." The devil is pictured as a cunning hunter (1 Peter 5:8). Using public criticism and the elder's own inconsistencies, the devil will entrap the unwary Christian into more serious sin – uncontrolled bitterness, angry retaliation, lying, further hypocrisy, and stubbornness of heart. What may begin as a small offense can become something far more destructive and evil. Therefore, an elder must have a good reputation with those outside the Christian community.

PRACTICAL QUESTIONS A POTENTIAL LEADER CAN ASK TO EVALUATE HIS OWN CHARACTER DEVELOPMENT.

1. Do I stay in close communion with the Holy Spirit?
2. Do I accept the Bible as the Word of God?
3. Do I love God's people?
4. Do I identify with God's people in a specific local church?
5. Do I willingly submit to authority?
6. Do I love the sinner and backslider?
7. Do I truly worship God with all of my heart?
8. Do I have a strong prayer life?
9. Do I have a mature attitude in pressure situations?
10. Do I let another person finish a job that I began without feeling any bitterness toward that person?
11. Do I listen to and receive criticism?
12. Do I accept it when someone else is assigned a job for which I am better qualified?
13. Do I gloat self-righteously when someone else makes a mistake?
14. Do I allow other people's opinions or do I always have to argue for my point of view?
15. Do I have inner peace during times of turmoil?
16. Do I forgive someone who deliberately ignores me?
17. Do I control my anger?
18. Do I pass up certain present pleasures to achieve long-term goals?
19. Do I finish the projects that I begin?
20. Do I put others before myself?
21. Do I face unpleasant disappointments without any bitterness?
22. Do I freely admit when I am wrong?
23. Do I keep my promises and complete my commitments?
24. Can I hold my tongue when it is best to do so?
25. Do I accept and live in peace with the things I cannot change?

CHAPTER 4
ETHICS IN PRACTICAL MINISTRY

THE MINISTER'S RELATIONSHIPS

While all relationships are important, the core relationships in ministers' lives should be given priority time, thought, and attention. Part of ministers' ethical responsibility involves cultivating enduring, enriching relationships with God, family, co-workers, and the congregation.

RELATIONSHIP WITH GOD

Ministers should engage in daily habits that foster a deep relationship with God. These habits go beyond perfunctory study and prayer. Intrinsic to the work of ministry is the intimate knowledge of God that comes only with time spent in God's presence. Ministers do well to learn as much as possible about their craft and calling, but the ethical center of ministry is the minister's personal relationship with God.

Deepening this relationship requires more than preparing the next presentation, but involves spending time alone with God with no agenda other than being with God. While each minister has to decide how to schedule this time, the discipline of doing so should be faithfully observed on a daily basis. Nothing will help ministers' love for self and others more effectively than a deepening relationship with God. To fail this responsibility is unethical both because it denies ministers' deepest needs and denies to those who depend on ministers for leadership the true source of spiritual health and vitality.

As their love for God grows, ministers' willingness to depend upon God also grows. 1 Peter 5:7 calls church leaders to "Cast all your anxiety on him, because He cares for you." Ministers who try to fix everyone and everything take on responsibilities which belong properly to God. Walking closely with God deepens self-understanding and builds the faith needed to turn problems over to the Holy Spirit. Depending upon God, ministers find the freedom to be themselves.

RELATIONSHIPS WITH FAMILY

Ministers' families can be encouragers, evaluators, healers, and sources of joy. Our families know us as no others, because what we are at home is most nearly what we are in truth. Because loving, healthy, grace-filled families accept us even as they know our faults, ministers need to understand and appropriate basic qualities that help shape healthy families.

One characteristic of healthy families is flexibility. Marriages face some of their greatest difficulties during times of change. The birth of children, kids starting school, job changes, and children leaving home are examples of stressful transitions. Many of these transitions, such as moving to another church or area of responsibility, can occur several times over the span of a minister's career, particularly for those who are part of more traditional mainline denominations. In many families both partners work outside of the home, and these transitions affect both spouses. Flexibility, support, and special consideration are important gifts family members can give one another during stressful transitional periods.

Another characteristic of healthy families is the encouragement of family members to be authentically themselves. Trying to make everyone fit the same mold is not only impossible but a mistake. Ministers' family members all have unique callings, and their lives should not simply revolve around ministers' lives. Finding the talents and spiritual gifts of each family member and encouraging one another to pursue those gifts is a sign of a healthy family and a healthy church.

The minister's own authenticity is crucial to cultivating and maintaining healthy relationships, especially at home. For example, if a minister's family members see a different person at church than they do at home, the quality of respect and depth of intimacy within the minister's family are sure to suffer.

RELATIONSHIPS WITH CO-WORKERS

A cooperative ministerial team is the product of both good intentions and hard work, and cooperation begins with a common philosophy of ministry. Ministers who cannot find common cause with the rest of the ministerial staff should consider relocating to a church more in tune with that minister's sense of calling, gifts, and understanding of ministry.

Once the staff basically agrees about philosophy of ministry, it is important to establish clear job descriptions and responsibilities. This is an ethical concern since fairness to each staff member requires clarity regarding goals and procedures for accurately measuring job performance.

Clarifying staff responsibilities is one aspect of a larger issue, communication. Difficulties tend to occur when adequate time and attention have not been devoted to building effective communication. An informal church staff tends to be a more cooperative church staff. Regular memos, phone calls, and meetings with other staff foster trust. So does discussing ideas and accepting opposing ideas in an open and respectful manner. Regular "clearing the air sessions" are far more preferable than allowing months of misunderstanding and potential bitterness to build up. Just as in family relationships, ignoring negative feelings tends to cause greater distress in the long run. Expressing positive and negative thoughts and feelings in loving and encouraging ways enhances staff relationships.

Some ministers feel the need to express their negative feelings about other church staff to church members. While doing so may make them feel better in the short run, these expectations undermine real communication and trust among staff members in the long run. Direct resolution of problems with other staff members is essential. The pain of hearing from a third or fourth party about a fellow staff member's discontent is detrimental to staff relationships and creates fissures not only in the staff, but also in the church body. Mustering the courage and integrity to work through problems directly and constructively with fellow staff members is foundational to healthy relationships.

When honest communication and appropriate confidentiality are practiced by ministerial co-workers, the door is opened to developing deeper and richer relationships. Trusting relationships among the church staff foster trusting relationships within the congregation.

RELATIONSHIPS WITH THE CONGREGATION
Respect and Love

Everyone wants to be loved, ministers being no exception. What is more rewarding and heartwarming than to be loved by an entire congregation, to be held close to their hearts, next to God and the beloved members of their immediate families? But as important as it may be for the minister to be loved, it is far more important to be respected. If the minister must sacrifice one or the other, he must at all costs maintain the parishioners' respect. Ministers should never be guilty of selling self-respect for mere affection. When ministers merit the respect of the people, but have not yet received their love, they will ultimately win their hearts by continuing to manifest godly love toward them. On the other hand, if ministers have gotten their love, but their ethics do not merit respect, they will not likely change the situation. True, the people's love for their minister will cover a "multitude of sins" (James 5:20), but without producing the esteem all ministers of God must have if they are to be effective leaders.

It is only right that ministers expect to have the highest ethical standard. It is not enough to be respected as a brother or sister in Christ; ministers must be examples, having set their hearts "on things above" (Col. 3:1).

Treating everyone with respect should be a goal for all ministers. Church members should know that their ministers genuinely care about and respect them. Respect is born out of the servant spirit which characterizes Christian ministry. As the apostle Paul affirms,

> **Philippians 2:3-4** (NKJV) [3] *Let* nothing *be done* through selfish ambition or conceit, but in lowliness of mind let each esteem others better than himself. [4] Let each of you look out not only for his own interests, but also for the interests of others.

Ultimately, love is the focus of all relationship ethics. Healthy relationships are loving relationships:

> **1 John 4:16** (NKJV) [16] And we have known and believed the love that God has for us. God is love, and he who abides in love abides in God, and God in him.

> **1 John 4:19-20** (NKJV) [19] We love Him because He first loved us. [20] If someone says, "I love God," and hates his brother, he is a liar; for he who does not love his brother whom he has seen, how can he love God whom he has not seen?

119

Keeping Confidence

There is no surer way for the minister to destroy the trust of a church member than to break confidence. Such a minister will not get a second chance. When approached by a member with a serious problem, the minister will not want to even hint that another member of the church has ever come with a similar problem. If the parishioner has requested confidentiality, the pastor should share the information with no one – usually not even his spouse.

The only situations wherein confidence cannot be held by ministers are to prevent a crime from taking place or to avoid becoming an accessory before the fact of a crime. Should the counselor sense that the confidence about to be shared involves criminal intent or action, the counselee should be interrupted and instructed that the counselor cannot keep such confidence. As William Rankin points out:

> There are certain kinds of situations clergy encounter in their roles as pastoral counselors that seem to lie close to, and perhaps beyond, the reach of confidentiality. The duty to keep a confidence is limited in cases where a dangerous person intends, or appears to intend, to commit acts of destruction. It is also limited when the pastor is being asked to cover up a crime, especially an ongoing crime. The alleged "privacy right" is not strongly and unambiguously supported in law, so this cannot always be regarded as a strong incentive to keep confidences in complex situations . . . Not even the initial promise to keep a confidence is an unyielding guarantee against future disclosure if the evidence suggests that innocent others may be made unduly vulnerably thereby – as in the tale of the child molester.[lviii]

Should the minister-counselor face the challenge of unwittingly receiving confidential information that involves the violation of the laws of the land or the clear teaching of Scripture, the minister must hold to the higher ethic of honoring God. James 5 and other biblical passages insist that the confessing of our faults is not for the cloaking of our transgressions, but rather to expose them so prayer can be offered, followed by forgiveness and healing.

Of course, sins of the past that have been dealt with or information that would bring harm or shame to others – these are exceptions. In the most complex situations the minister will find divine guidance by holding to divine guidelines; in dealing with confidential information, the same untainted premise that was established centuries ago in the writing of the prophet still pertains – "steadfast love, justice, and righteousness" (Jer. 9:24, NRS). Hopefully, ministers will behave so appropriately that parishioners will know they can trust their minister as a keeper of confidences, one who will be faithful to them as well as to God, one they will not burden with compromising information.

FOR THE MINISTER:

- I will foster my relationship and dependence upon God.

- I will act in loving and respectful ways toward my family and work through every challenge to enrich my relationships with each family member.

- I will act in loving and respectful ways toward my church family and work through every challenge to enrich my relationships with each church member.

- I will nurture good communications with all staff members, treat them with respect, keep their communications confidential, bear their burdens in prayer, and seek to encourage their ministries.

121

- I will treat others according to the spirit and letter of Jesus' teaching (e.g., "*In everything, do to others as you would have them do to you; for this is the law and the prophets*" Matt. 7:12).

FOR THE CHURCH:
- We will be guided by the conviction that our ministers serve with us in God's service and are not "hired help" to do ministry.

- We will respect our ministers' unique gifts, callings, and personalities as we encourage them to excellence.

- We will respect the importance of ministers' families and honor each family member.

- We will commit to develop and nurture strong relationships within the congregation and show that we are Christians by our love.

STEWARDSHIP OF TIME

The large clock situated in the towering steeple of a Dallas church is inscribed with the warning, "*Night Cometh*." The haunting inscription is based on Jesus' familiar teaching in the Fourth Gospel:

> **John 9:4-5** (NKJV) [4] I must work the works of Him who sent Me while it is day; *the* night is coming when no one can work. [5] As long as I am in the world, I am the light of the world."

The symbol of the clock and scripture reminds ministers about the stewardship of time in the context of the call to ministry. Ministers are all too familiar with the brevity of time as they deal with the endless demands of ministry. Night comes all too quickly, and at the end of each day ministers are left to ponder how faithfully they have fulfilled their mission of doing God's work.

The busy work of keeping people happy drains ministers of direction and purpose. In addition, the ever-flowing stream of pastoral tasks remains constant as ministers respond to one more request, phone call, visit, meeting, preparation, or unexpected crisis. Ministers find it difficult to place a comma, let alone a period, at the end of the day. Everything seems so unfinished in pastoral ministry.

THE GIFT OF TIME

Ministers lose sight of the gift of time by living exclusively in what the Greeks called *chronos* time. This chronological sense of time calculates its passage by filling out a daily planner. In *chronos* time, events unfold one after the other, like a perennial passing of seasons. Ecclesiastes captures the tendency of *chronos* time to become repetitious and routine:

Ecclesiastes 1:3-5 (NKJV) [3] What profit has a man from all his labor In which he toils under the sun? [4] *One* generation passes away, and *another* generation comes; But the earth abides forever. [5] The sun also rises, and the sun goes down, And hastens to the place where it arose.

Another sense of time is captured by the Greek word *kairos*. In the New Testament, *kairos* denotes a moment of opportunity and this fills life with possibility, potential, and new perspective. Paul speaks of *kairos* time in his letter to the Galatians: "But when the time had fully come, God sent His Son" (Gal. 4:4). In this *kairos* moment, all of time takes on new meaning as Jesus Christ enters time and space. Time now offers the possibility of God invading ordinary moments with sacred presence. The holiness of each day provides a "wake-up call" that says, "Handle this day with care." The scripture signals its own alarm:

> **Ephesians 5:14** (NKJV) [14] Therefore He says: "Awake, you who sleep, Arise from the dead, And Christ will give you light."

SELF- MANAGEMENT, NOT TIME MANAGEMENT

While time management books, daily organizers, and quick-fix seminars promise solutions for the unpredictable schedules of ministers, the answer for solving time issues does not rest in management techniques. Ministers become faithful stewards of time only when they remember that time is a gift from God. As the Psalmist proclaims, "*My times are in your hand*" (Ps. 31:15).

The stewardship of time grows out of understanding the minister's purpose as a messenger of reconciliation (2 Cor. 5:19-20). Ministers confront the challenge of this purpose with requests prefaced by the observation, "I know you are so busy." Ministers find it hard not to take this remark as a compliment as it makes them feel both in demand and worthy of their hire. Yet interpreting the stewardship of time in terms of sheer busyness is as lethal as it is seductive. Eventually, business leads to burnout.

John Wesley commented on the trap of busyness in his remark, "We have no time to hurry." Instead of simply being busy, ministers' lives and schedules need to reflect their divinely driven purpose rather than being merely directed by clock and calendar. Wise ministers travel with a compass, which enables them to interpret the priorities of ministry. These ministers consult the compass of God's Word, the direction of prayer, and the leadership of the Holy Spirit in determining decisions regarding time.

The minister's use of time demands discipline. Broken trust includes more than sexual misconduct or dishonesty. Even though ministers are chronically pressed for time, a certain degree of flexibility exists within the minister's schedule. During the week ministers usually work alone in their offices out of sight of congregation or supervisor. No two days are the same. Definite tasks fill part of each week, but significant segments of time exists within the minister's own discretion. For instance, ministers who have preaching or teaching responsibilities have a choice about the use of time. They can discipline themselves with faithful hours of preparation, or misuse their preparation time and throw together sermons or lessons at the last minute. Jesus' rebuke to the unfaithful servant in the Parable of the Talents, "You wicked and lazy servant," (Matt. 25:26) also warns ministers who invest their time poorly. The indictment of the ministers who squanders time compares to the banker who embezzles funds or the corrupt accounting practices of corporate executives.

STEWARDSHIP OF TIME BEFORE GOD

Ministers cannot depend on external controls, whether these take the form of demanding church members or relentless deadlines. Ultimately, ministers are accountable to God; inward obedience to Jesus Christ controls the ethical minister's choices concerning the use of time. Paul frames the stewardship of time for the whole church: "*For we are what He has made us, created in Christ Jesus for good works, which God prepared beforehand to be our way of life*" (Eph. 2:10).

The ethics of ministers' use of time includes faithfully meeting deadlines and honoring commitments rather than succumbing to procrastination. On the other side of the time equation, the Sabbath principle calls ministers to set aside time for prayer and spiritual formation. The proverbial saying, "The bow that is always bent fails to shoot straight" finds validation in Jesus' instruction to the disciples: "*He said to them, 'Come away to a deserted place all by yourselves and rest a while*" (Mark 6:31). Finally, quality family time must not be allowed to substitute for quantity of family time. The minister's ethics of time, whether leading people to faith or spending time with his or her family, finds direction in Paul's counsel, *"Be careful then how you live, not as unwise but as the wise, making the most of the time"* (Eph. 5:15-16a).

FOR THE MINISTER:

- I will live in gratitude for the gift of time and the ways in which God redeems our time in Jesus Christ (Eph. 5:15-16a).

- I will be committed to the good stewardship of time. I will be disciplined in my use of time, which includes not wasting time or working at all times.

- I will be faithful in my use of time by honoring my commitments, being faithful to my promises, and being diligent in study (Matt. 5:37; 2 Tim. 2:15).

- I will recognize that God is Creator, time is finite, and there are limits to what I can humanly accomplish in ministry (Acts 14:11-15).

- I will honor the Sabbath principle by regularly taking time off for rest and re-creation (Gen. 2:2-3).

- I will provide for my family by taking time to nurture and support our relationship (1 Tim. 5:8).

FOR THE CHURCH:

- We will recognize ministers' need for rest and time to be away from work. We will protect their time to have a day off and their family time.

- We will provide time and financial support for study, continuing education, and refreshment away from pastoral duties.

- We affirm the concept that "every member is a minister" and will not expect the pastoral staff to always be on call.

- We will encourage our staff to know the difference between a true pastoral crisis and a need which can wait until a more appropriate time.

THE MINISTER'S HEALTH

Jesus spoke to the first disciples about life and life "*to the full*" (John 10:10). While the allusion is more to quality of life, some readers unfortunately construe Jesus' point as having little to do with physical life. Although the New Testament does not provide a strict guideline for ministers to be healthy, the implication toward health is at least implied in God's perfect creation. Matthew 5:48 and 1 Peter 1:16 call us toward holy perfection. Is this admonition only applicable to spiritual matters? If this were the case, then God's holiness would not extend beyond the spiritual. The New Testament also calls us to be good stewards of God's gifts, and health is clearly one of God's most precious gifts.

In fact, a close reading of 2 Timothy 2:3-7 reveals pastoral concern for Timothy's physical health. This passage shows an appreciation for the importance of physical and mental conditioning. Jesus' miracles of healing and of the multiplication of the fish and loaves demonstrate God's concern for physical life. In the Sermon on the Mount, Jesus confirms the legitimacy of our physical needs: "*your heavenly Father knows that you need all these things*" (Matt. 6:25-33). According to Paul, the Christian's body is a temple of the Holy Spirit and intended to glorify God (1 Cor. 6:19-20). We are psychosomatic beings; that is, our mental/emotional selves are integrated with our physical selves. We are responsible to God for how we live the totality of our lives.

Ministers should be attentive to their bodies. To know ourselves means to have a realistic assessment of physical and emotional health. The following questions can be helpful in moving toward healthy self-knowledge:

How Do I Think?

Ministers need periodically to examine how they access, process, and apply thoughts. This self-examination is important because the moral life can be depicted roughly as the combination of convictions, attitudes, and actions which we display throughout our lives. A simpler way to make the same point is that our mind-style shapes our lifestyle. The New Testament (e.g., 2 Cor. 10:5; Phil. 4:1-9; Col. 3:5-10; 1 Pet. 5:7-8) is quite clear that thought life is important – so important as to affect overall health. Implicitly and explicitly, these passages demonstrate functional, strategic, and tactical methods to address thought life.

For centuries, Christians have observed practices for developing their inner selves. These exercises, sometimes called spiritual disciplines, engage mind, body, and spirit. Meditation, prayer, fasting, study, simplicity, solitude, submission, service, confession, worship, guidance, and celebration form a foundation of disciplines which are also checks and balances that greatly enhance ministers' health. Some form of spiritual direction, whether through a spiritual director, accountability group, or peer group, can foster spiritual formation, emotional maturity, and honest self-awareness.

How Do I Eat?

Obesity remains a national problem. Junk food diets, high fat and high sugar content foods, and inattention to the impact of what we eat or don't eat have made a society-wide impact. Some recent reports place the percentage of obese people in America as high as 60 percent. This trend is widely noticeable among ministers. Since ministers are called with the rest of the church to be good stewards of their bodies, gluttony detracts from their public and private witness to the Gospel. Unhealthy eating habits negatively affect ministers' general health, as well as health care and insurance costs. Proverbs 23:1-2 should graphically draws their attention to the need to monitor what and how they eat.

WHAT ABOUT REST, RECREATION, AND EXERCISE?

Medical research demonstrates that sleep deprivation – low quality sleep – negatively affects health. Many ministers tend to over work, without sufficient recognition of the Sabbath principle for their lives. Sabbath, instituted in creation (Gen. 2:2) and articulated in the Ten Commandments (Exodus 20:8-10), stands as a guideline for all Christians. For their own sakes and as a model for their congregation, ministers need to implement a Sabbath pattern of re-creation. A certain egocentrism can develop as ministers come to believe that the work of God's Kingdom depends solely on human effort.

What applies to all of creation clearly applies to ministers; *all of us* need to take a deliberative approach to the rest-work cycle. Observing the Sabbath principle positively impacts every level of existence – physical, emotional, and spiritual.

The pace of contemporary life for many ministers tends to impede getting enough physical exercise. Stress-induced conditions, fatigue, and even mild depression can be alleviated or minimized through regular, individually appropriate exercise. Abundant resources are readily available for ministers to establish exercise regimens which fit their needs.

TO WHAT AM I ADDICTED?

Addictive patterns of life are not limited to drug abuse and other kinds of substance abuse. In his book *Celebration of Discipline*, Richard Foster advises Christians to refrain from *anything* which leads to addictive patterns in our lives. As important as the work of professional ministers may be to the Kingdom of God, ministerial duties can lapse into "workaholism." As nurturing as family relationships are to all of us, even our families can become too much the focus of our lives. As necessary as food and recreation were to our health, these too can become inappropriately important. Whatever is becoming an idol, i.e., the controlling center of our lives other than God in Christ, should be resisted.

WHEN WAS MY LAST MEDICAL CHECKUP?

Getting regular medical check-ups is an important act of stewardship of ministers' health. Heart disease, strokes, and cancer rank at the top of physical maladies which plague American society, and many of these conditions can be prevented and/or effectively treated by regular visits with a physician. Since vocational ministry can be highly stressful and stress tends to aggravate health problems, it is especially important for ministers to practice preventative medicine.

CONCLUSION

Ministers may say, "There is so much to do, and I don't have time to implement the health practices suggested here." The appropriate response is that ministers do not have time not to implement these suggestions. Some of the finest years of ministry should come in the fifties, sixties, and beyond when experience, wisdom, and years of having walked with God bear abundant fruit. Yet, physical problems that could have been prevented with preemptive and preventative care rob many ministers of their most productive decades of life. Inherent within the calling to vocational ministry is a stewardship of the totality of life with which God has gifted us. Faithful stewardship in this regard enhances the authenticity and integrity of our lives.

FOR THE MINISTER:
- I will recognize the interdependence of my mind and body and God's calling, offering the totality of my being "*as a living sacrifice. . . to God*" (Rom. 12:1-2).

- I will be both accountable and faithful to God regarding my stewardship of the good gift of health.

- I will make a serious commitment toward the disciplines of spiritual and physical formation, including appropriate physical exercise.

- I will honestly face the question, "Does my mind-style and lifestyle reflect the integrity of the Gospel at work in my personality and life?"

FOR THE CHURCH:
- We will recognize our own and our ministers' needs for spiritual formation and physical well-being.

- We will commit ourselves to mutual accountability before God regarding spiritual and physical development.

- We will involve ourselves in witnessing to a holistic Gospel in which our whole selves are undergoing redemption.

ECONOMIC RESPONSIBILITIES

Ministers are called to engage the full expanse of human

relationships and responsibilities, including the critically important area of economic life. The significance of economic responsibility is underwritten by two realities. First is the central place of economic responsibility in scripture. In the Sermon on the Mount (Matt. 5-7), Jesus teaches His followers to not "*store up treasures on earth*" (Matt. 6:19) and that no one can serve two masters: "*you cannot serve God and wealth*" (Matt. 6:24). He teaches His followers first to seek God's Kingdom and righteousness "*and all these things will be given you as well*" (Matt. 6:33). 1st Timothy 6:7-10 warns Christians concerning the dangers of money and possessions with the admonition that "*those who want to be rich fall into temptation and are trapped by many senseless and harmful desires that plunge people into ruin and destruction*" (1 Tim. 6:9). The love of wealth is one of the most frequently identified spiritual dangers in scripture.

Second is the reality of contemporary clergy living and ministering within a materialistic and consumer-driven culture. Caught between these two realities, ministers find themselves trying to cope with cultural influences while proclaiming in word and deed the dangers of one of culture's most obvious idolatries.

THE FAILURE OF ECONOMIC RESPONSIBILITY

Plenty of evidence demonstrates how religious leaders have failed at this task by engaging in manipulation and misrepresentation to advance their financial interest. Some of the more common and well-documented economic frauds perpetrated by some religious leaders include embezzlements, investment scams, misappropriation of funds, and income-tax evasion. [lix] Clearly, ministers need to be good stewards of their personal financial resources as well as the church's wealth.

Less-documented, but equally destructive, are several other issues regarding economic ethics. Conflicts of interest can arise when ministers become financially indebted to church members or others in their communities. Some clergy are tempted to maintain lifestyles for themselves and their families that mirror the lifestyles of affluent members of their congregations. In other cases, poor financial planning can lead to indebtedness that is both a burden and a poor example of Christian stewardship. In this context it is important to acknowledge that not every incident of crushing debt is the result of poor planning. Even one health crisis can lead to mounting debt, and any number of other crises can and do financially impact ministers' lives. Like other professionals whose careers entail various levels of higher education, ministers often finish their formal training with the burden of large student loans.

Another important issue is how much ministers should give to the church and other worthy causes. Some excuse minimal offerings by claiming that they are giving their entire lives to the church. While many variables influence how much ministers can and should give, the point remains that ministers should be generous stewards of financial and other resources. They should also provide the example for the rest of the congregation.

The temptation for religious leaders to use their power and influence to secure wealth is an ancient problem. In 1 Samuel the story of the sons of Eli begins, "*Now the sons of Eli were scoundrels*" (1 Sam. 2:12). The narrative clarifies this judgment by explaining that the priests (i.e., the sons of Eli) would send their servants to take, by force if necessary, meat that had been offered as a sacrifice to God for the priests' own consumption. The gravity of this offense is made clear by describing how the priests were satisfying their greed by grasping for that which was being presented to God: "*they treated the offerings of the Lord with contempt*" (1 Sam. 12:17). They were stealing from God and from the faithful who had given to God.

VOWS OF POVERTY?

At the other end of the spectrum are ministers who, along with their families, suffer from inadequate income. Recent studies reveal that this problem is quite common, especially in denominations with congregational-style organizations.[ix] A 2003 survey conducted by Duke University's Divinity School reveals that the median annual pay (including the value of any free housing) for Protestant ministers is $40,000. However, 60 percent of Protestant pastors serving small churches with congregational governments receive a median income of $22,300. A co-director of the survey concluded, *"Protestants' free-market approach forces clergy to compete for bigger, higher-paying congregations, turning the ministry from a 'calling' into a mere 'career.'"*[lxi] In these cases, churches that can afford to provide adequate compensation to their ministers need to be challenged to meet their responsibility. If paying adequate wages is not possible because of a church's size or financial status, ministers and churches should consider the move toward bi-vocational ministry. Part of ministers' and churches' success in making this transition involves affirming the status of bi-vocational ministry as both competent and faithful.

In his sermon, *The Use of Money*, John Wesley contended that Christians should *"gain all you can, save all you can, and give all you can."* Wesley thus avoids both the view that money in inherently evil and the correlative notion that a vow of poverty is an essential part of the minister's call. He goes on to warn that in gaining wealth, Christians should neither harm one's neighbor nor one's spiritual integrity. The change to save all you can reminds us that we are not to spend all we can. Wesley contends that Christians should be frugal and consume only what "plain nature" requires. At the same time, we should be especially alert to the reality that being appropriately satisfied can overcome inordinate desires.

The call to give all we can explains the reason for gaining and saving. This call is a reminder that we are not *proprietors but stewards*. Responsible ministers should commit their wealth to meeting the needs of those for whom they are immediately responsible (1 Tim. 5:8) and then, as resources and opportunities allow, the needs of humanity. Along with every other member of the congregation, ministers bear the responsibility to financially support the ministries of the church with their tithes and offerings. In so giving, ministers can bear witness to a responsible stewardship of wealth.

John Richard Neuhaus reminds ministers that

> ...most do not "sell out" by making crooked deals, or even by consciously compromising principle in order not to compromise financial security; we pay our tribute to Mammon in the minutes and hours spent in worrying about money and the things that money can get . . . [T]he question of money and the dangers it poses should be kept under the closest scrutiny. Otherwise the desire ineluctably grows, avarice feeds upon itself, and one ends up as the victim of an appetite that is in fact insatiable and consumes by worry, guilt, and discontent the hours and days that were once consecrated to ministry.[lxii]

John Wesley's attempt to strike a balance between avarice and austerity suggests a practical and positive pattern for contemporary ministerial ethics. Ministers should remember that obsession with money, whether in grasping for too much or worrying about too little, can become a corrosive spiritual poison. As Proverbs teaches,

> **Proverbs 30:8-9** (NKJV) [8] Remove falsehood and lies far from me; Give me neither poverty nor riches— Feed me with the food allotted to me; [9] Lest I be full and deny *You,* And

say, "Who *is* the LORD?" Or lest I be poor and steal, and profane the name of my God.

FOR THE MINISTER:
- I will be honest in my stewardship of money.

- I will live within my income and not become hampered by unpaid debts.

- I will exercise a lifestyle consistent with the life and teachings of Christ.

- I will not seek special gratuities, privileges, bequest, or loans because of my role as minister.

- I will not become involved in funeral or marriage schemes (or any other schemes) that seek to profit from the performance of my ministerial duties.

- I will advocate adequate financial compensation for my profession including the entire church staff.

- I will be generous in my stewardship of money, contributing to the ministries of the church and the needs of humanity with my tithes and offerings.

FOR THE CHURCH:
- We will practice good stewardship in a spirit of kindness and generosity.

- We understand that workers are "worthy of their hire" and will compensate with fairness and generosity.

- We will stay aware of rising costs for insurance and other living expenses in our culture and plan our compensation accordingly.

- We will not become "enablers" of a minister's poor habits or poor discipline by making loans or gifts beyond reason or extenuating circumstances.

- We will also offer help by way of financial counseling and mentoring if needed, but will not pry into the private matters of our ministers.

SEXUAL CONDUCT

One of the most destructive failures by clergy is sexual misconduct. The damage caused by this failure spreads like a virus throughout the church, devastating families and individuals.

EXTENT OF THE PROBLEM

Sexual failures are often headline news, implicating clergy in all religious bodies. Careful studies over several decades have attempted to understand both the causes and extent of the problem. In one study questionnaires were sent to 1000 Baptist pastors in six Southern states. Of those responding, 14.1 percent acknowledged inappropriate sexual contact in their ministries; 70.4 percent said they knew of some other minister's sexual failings; and 24.2 percent reported that they had counseled at least one person who claimed to have had sexual contact with a minister.[lxiii] Other studies indicate similar results among clergy within a wide range of religious groups.[lxiv] *Broken Trust*, a resource for churches dealing with clergy sexual misconduct published by the Texas Baptist Christian Life Commission, identified four expressions of sexual misconduct by ministers: sexual relations outside of marriage; unwanted or inappropriate physical contact; other sexually oriented or suggestive behaviors, including sexually suggestive speech and gestures; and the use of pornography.[lxv]

The problem of ministerial sexual misconduct is not just a modern problem, but has plagued the people of God throughout history. Problems with or arising from improper sexual relationships are reflected in the stories of Abraham, Lot, Samson, David, and Solomon. And in this context as well, the sons of Eli are described as "scoundrels" (1 Sam. 2:12):

> **1 Samuel 2:22-23** (NKJV) [22] Now Eli was very old; and he heard everything his sons did to all Israel, and how they lay with the women who assembled at the door of the tabernacle of meeting. [23] So he said to them, "Why do you do such things? For I hear of your evil dealings from all the people.

EXPRESSION OF THE PROBLEM

Eli's question continues to haunt us. Recent studies suggest that there are at least four contributing factors.

Abuse of power seems to be the most prevalent factor in clergy sexual misconduct. [lxvi] In a culture in which a dominant understanding of sexual relations is conquest, clergy are tempted to use their status and power to conquer sexually.

Sexual addiction is increasingly recognized as a factor in inappropriate behaviors of ministers.[lxvii] Compulsive behaviors are often the result of a serious personality disorder in which there is a recurrent failure to control behaviors even in the face of undesirable consequences. One of the deep tragedies of sexual addiction is that many affected ministers seem to have entered the ministry in the attempt to overcome their addictive tendencies.

A third factor is the *misinterpretation of intimate relationships.*[lxviii]

Many clergy relationships, especially counseling relationships, involve some degree of intimacy. A recurring temptation is to allow such relationships to extend beyond appropriate boundaries.

Stress or *"burnout"* is a common experience for ministers. Weakened by exhaustion, clergy become more vulnerable to temptation. This causal factor was identified as prevalent in the study of misconduct of Baptist pastors cited above.[lxix]

DEALING WITH SEXUALITY

Prevention is the first defense against the damage inflicted by sexual misconduct, and ministers can take several basic steps to enhance prevention:

1. Ministers must understand that they are called to be servants, not rulers. The power is a gift from God to be used in healing, not in conquering.

2. Ministers must nurture and protect their family life. Honest discussions of sexual needs with spouses are essential. Counseling may be needed, and ministers and their spouses should not be stigmatized for availing themselves of therapeutic help.

3. Ministers should observe stated standards regarding boundaries in counseling and other forms of pastoral ministry to minimize misinterpretations and temptations.

4. Ministers must be aware of their own hearts, their own vulnerabilities and their strengths, and must nurture a deep relationship with God. Extra-marital sexual sins are not only against the spouse, the partner, the family, and the church, but also violate our relationship with the Lord.

5. Careful attention to the biblical admonitions concerning sexual conduct and misconduct can help ministers through times of weakness and vulnerability. Ministers must not allow rationalizing, denial, compromising, or justifying to cloud their vision of the biblical standard of faithfulness in marriage and celibacy in singleness.

6. Having a trusted friend or mentor with whom confidentiality is assured, truth is forthrightly spoken, and accountability is held high will also help ministers to live faithfully.

7. Ministers should focus not only on sexual sins, but also on the truth that our sexuality is a gift from God. The minister's task is to proclaim by word and deed that we are to be good stewards of this good gift through and within the intimacy of marriage.

FOR THE MINISTER:
- I will recognize that sexuality is God's gift, which can be used for both good and evil.

- I will clearly demonstrate a life of sexual fidelity and integrity in all of my relationships and a steadfast commitment to the biblical standard of faithfulness in marriage and celibacy in singleness.

- I will not allow sexuality to become the driving force of any of my relationships.

- I will establish and observe appropriate boundaries in pastoral ministry.

- I will commit myself to constructive counseling in the event that my sexuality is expressed inappropriately.

FOR THE CHURCH:
- We recognize we are sexual beings before God and that our sexuality is an arena for Christian witness and discipleship.

- We will commit ourselves to exhibiting wholesome sexual relationships among ourselves, within our families, and beyond the church family.

- We will commit ourselves to forming relationships, time structures, and ministry activities so that our ministers can build wholesome family relationships.

THE MINISTER AND THE COMMUNITY

Effective, responsible ministers see their churches as integral parts of the community. The false dichotomy of "us" versus "them" between church and community gives way to the realization that "we" are "them."

Jesus taught His followers to be salt and light in the world: "*Let your light shine before others, so that they may see your good works and give glory to your Father in heaven*" (Matt. 5:16). Implicit in Jesus' teaching is that the good deeds that bring glory to God should be done in the community. Jesus also told the disciples that others would identify His followers by the love they had for one another. This is to say the central ideas of unity and community were built into the framework of discipleship. Jesus involved Himself in the community – at weddings, dinners, healings, feedings, and funerals. The Gospels confirm that Jesus went to these events not to "show off," but to meet the people's needs in the very places where they gathered. Effective and ethical ministers will do the same in their own communities both through their personal involvement and through the involvement of their church families.

The apostle Paul encourages community building, involvement, and meeting needs and doing so with the highest of ethical standards (Phil. 4:8-10; Col. 3:5-11). In fact, every Pauline epistle appeals directly or indirectly for conduct befitting the name and nature of Christ. Paul affirms Jesus' depiction of His followers as *"in the world, but not of the world"* (cf. John 17:15-16) and expresses the communal scope of this image.

Throughout the scope of Christian history, churches have related to their communities in a variety of ways, ranging from total non-involvement to total absorption. Ethical and effective ministers attempt to strike a healthy balance between involvement and distinctiveness by discovering ways of connecting with the world. This balance may include prayer and working for the community to adopt more Christ-like attitudes and actions (e.g., regarding race relations, gambling, substance abuse, sexual morality, business ethics, and social justice). Ministers should also relate to people in the community on very human levels (e.g., school plays and concerts, local sports teams, community theatre, local politics).

Ministers who involve themselves and their churches in the community open several doors from which the gospel may move into the life of the community and the community can come into the life of the church. As ministers involve themselves with their communities, they discover issues on the hearts and minds of the people. They also see critical ministries that churches are uniquely positioned to provide (e.g., addiction/recovery groups, clothes closets, food pantries, prison ministries, Habitat for Humanity, business chaplaincy) and community activities that churches may choose to house or sponsor (e.g., civic clubs, sports leagues, community theatre and arts development, PTA groups, cultural activities, and senior groups).

It is at these levels of connecting with people, their needs, and their interests that the church is most relevant and alive in embodying the love of Christ. Ministers who closely follow the way of Jesus not only acquire skill in preaching, writing, witnessing, planning, and leading, but also connect deeply with the hearts and hurts of broken people in a broken world. Community involvement is an arena in which the skills of preaching, teaching, witnessing, planning and leading are polished with the grit of reality and so reflect brightly the Light of the world.

FOR MINISTERS AND CHURCHES:

- We will value the larger community beyond the reference points of our local congregation, reaching out to people who may never be members of our church and caring about important issues which may not directly impact our church members.

- We shall endeavor to know and be known in the communities that we serve as witnesses to the love of Christ, who meets physical, emotional, and spiritual needs.

- We shall look deeply into the communities in which we serve to understand and minister to their needs and concerns and to rejoice in their triumphs.

COVENANT OF MINISTERIAL ETHICS

SUMMATION

The covenant of Ministerial Ethics calls ministers to the life-long commitment of integrity and wholeness in Jesus Christ and to "live as children of light" (Eph. 4:8-14) as they serve God and their congregations. The covenant affirms that credibility and effectiveness in ministry is primarily built on the faithfulness and trustworthiness of the minister (2 Timothy 2:15).

The preceding essay, on ministerial ethics provide biblical and theological foundations, address crucial areas of ministerial ethics, and offer guidance and direction for coping with the ethical demands of ministry. At the conclusion of the essays addressing specific ethical concerns are covenants of accountability which focus on relevant commitments for ministers and congregations. The essays and covenants provide material for further reflection and can serve as a resource for discussion between ministers and congregations.

The following Covenant of Ministerial Ethics condenses the preceding essays and biblical material into a framework for living and ministering with ethical integrity. We strongly encourage ministers to sign this covenant and use it as a guide for their lives and work. We urge that a signed copy of the covenant be kept by the minister and distributed to church leaders. We suggest that the church publish the covenant as a way of cultivating confidence that the ministers of the church are committed to integrity and accountability in their lives and ministries.

THEOLOGICAL FOUNDATION

Berith, the Hebrew word for covenant, is one of the key words and concepts in scripture. It appears at least 286 times in the Old

Testament and is a central unifying theme in the Bible. The basic biblical meaning of covenant is a contract, a pact, a promise, alliance, or agreement which binds together the covenanting parties.

One of the distinguishing characteristics of God in scripture is displayed in the stories of God's determination to enter into covenants with humankind. In Genesis 9, God covenants with Noah (Gen. 9:9-17) with the divine promise never to repeat the flood. A few chapters later, God enters into solemn covenant with Abraham (Gen. 15:18; 17:2), promising land, descendants, and a blessing. In the New Testament, Jesus uses the bread and the cup at the last supper as symbols of the new covenant embodied in His life, death, and resurrection.

Covenants always entail responsibilities for at least one of the covenant partners. The people of Israel were called by God in Exodus 19:4-6 to "*obey My voice and keep My covenants.*" Then the people would be "*My treasured possession . . . a priestly kingdom . . . a holy nation.*" Ministers and the congregations they serve accept similar responsibilities of faithfulness and blessings as churches seek to minister in Jesus' name.

The concept of faithfulness is deeply connected to covenant (Jer. 14:21). The word faithful – which means steadfast, dedicated, dependable, and worthy of trust – is used to describe the relationship between God and Israel (Deut. 7:9): "*God . . . maintains covenant loyalty with those who love Him and keep His commandments.*" In 1 Corinthians 7:25 Paul offers pastoral counsel to the Corinthian congregation as a "*trustworthy*" minister.

Built upon fidelity, the covenant between ministers and congregations is not a static code, but a living and dynamic relationship. Jeremiah describes the internal nature of such a covenant, which is its heart and soul: "*The days are surely coming, says the LORD, when I will make a new covenant with the house of*

146

Israel and the house of Judah . . . I will put my law within them, and I will write it on their hearts; and I will be their God, and they shall be my people" (Jer. 31:31, 33).

A Covenant of Ministerial Ethics moves beyond external restraints, like rules posted on the employee bulletin board, to the incarnation of ministerial integrity in relationships. Authentic, Christian ministry develops and nurtures healthy relationships between ministers and congregations. The standard by which ministers and congregations should be measured is not secular success, but by faithfulness to the covenant of ministerial ethics and the relationships which are the fruit of covenant fidelity.

PREAMBLE

As a minister of the gospel of Jesus Christ, called by God's grace through God's providence and purpose for my life and gifted by the Spirit for equipping the church, I commit myself to incarnate the biblical understanding of ministry and the ethical precepts that are contained in this covenant, in order that my ministry might faithfully reflect Jesus' life, death, and resurrection. As the congregation served by this minister, we commit ourselves to embody the promises contained in this covenant so that we might faithfully reflect the way of Jesus in our ministry to one another and to the world.

FOR THE MINISTER:

- I will reflect the integrity of the Gospel of Jesus Christ in my ministry by leading the congregation to follow Jesus, so becoming the salt of the earth and the light of the world, loving our enemies, becoming agents of reconciliation, doing justice for "the least of these," speaking the truth in love, loving God as we love one another, and serving God as we serve one another.

- I will respond to the call of Christ with faithful obedience and count it a joyful privilege to be asked to serve in ministry.

- I will be intentional in nurturing relationships with family, friends, colleagues, and members of the congregation. I recognize the importance of building healthy relationships which are both open and honest and free from coercion, deception, manipulation, and the abuse of the power of my position.

- I will be committed to the faithful stewardship of time. I will be disciplined in my use of time, which includes not wasting time or working at all times. I will take time for spiritual formation, study, prayer, and rest.

- I will develop a healthy lifestyle which includes my spiritual, physical, and emotional health.

- I will be financially responsible, which responsibility includes paying my bills, avoiding financial favors, living within my salary, contributing to the financial support of my church and other ministries, and adopting a lifestyle consistent with biblical teachings concerning possessions and money.

- I will clearly demonstrate a life of sexual fidelity and integrity in all of my relationships and a commitment to the biblical standard of faithfulness in marriage and celibacy in singleness.

- I will participate in the larger community as the context of my ministry. I will be committed to the issues of justice, compassion, reconciliation, and to the marginalized as I value all of God's children.

- I will be directed in all that I do by Jesus' vision in the model prayer: *"Thy Kingdom come, Thy will be done on earth as it is in heaven."* I will be dedicated to God's sovereign role and reign in every area of my life and be faithful in announcing that God's Kingdom has come in Jesus Christ.

FOR THE CHURCH:

- We will honor and respect the call of God in the lives of our ministers and count their service among us as a gift from God.

- We will commit ourselves to forming relationships, time structures, and ministry activities so that our ministers can build wholesome family relationships.

- We will respect our ministers' families and honor them as vital parts of our ministry team.

- We will commit to develop and nurture strong relationships within the congregation and show we are Christian by our love.

- We will recognize our ministers' need for rest and time to be away from work. We will protect their time to have a day off and their family time.

- We will recognize our own and our ministers' needs for spiritual formation and physical well-being.

- We understand that workers are "worthy of their hire" and will compensate ministers with fairness and generosity.

- We will commit ourselves to exhibiting faithful and wholesome sexual relationships among ourselves, within our families, and beyond the church family.

- We shall endeavor to know and be known in the communities that we serve as witnesses to the love of Christ, who meets physical, emotional, and spiritual needs.

MINISTER

_____

Name

_____

Signature

_____

Date

CHURCH REPRESENTATIVE

_____

Name

_____

Signature

_____

Date

END NOTES:

[i]G.W. Bromiley, "Philosophical Ethics: Nature and Function," *The International Standard Bible Encyclopedia* (Grand Rapids, Michigan: Eerdmans, reprinted 1988) Vol. 2, p. 167.

[ii]D. Elton Trueblood, *Philosophy of Religion* (Grand Rapids, Michigan: Baker, 1975), p. 111.

[iii]Leander S. Keyser, *A Manual of Christian Ethics* (Burlington, Ia: The Lutheran Literary Board, 1926), p. 31.

[iv]George Walker, *The Idealism of Christian Ethics* (Baird Lecture, 1928 Edinburgh: T. & T. Clark Co., 1929), p. 30.

[v]Carl F.H. Henry, *Christian Personal Ethics* (Grand Rapids, Michigan: Wm. B. Eerdmans Publishing Co., 1957), p. 210.

[vi]David A. Noebel, *Understanding the Times* (Manitou Spring, Colorado: Summit Press, 1992), p. 238.

[vii]Dietrich Bonhoeffer, *Ethics* with Eberhard Bethge, ed. (New York: Macmillan, 1986), p. 84.

[viii]W. G. D. MacLennan, *Christian Obedience* (London: Thomas Nelson and Sons Ltd., 1948), p. 100.

[ix]G.C. Adolph von Harless, *System of Christian Ethics,* (Edinburgh: T. & T. Clark., 1887), p. 63.

[x]Henry op. cit. pp. 217-218.

[xi]MacLennan, op. cit. pp. 16, 18.

[xii]Roger R. Nicole, "Authority," in Carl F.H. Henry, ed., *Baker's Dictionary of Christian Ethics* (Grand Rapids, Michigan: Baker Book House, 1973), p. 47.

[xiii]Henry, op. cit. p. 213.

[xiv]*Webster's II New Riverside University Dictionary* (Boston, Massachusetts: The Riverside Publishing Company, 1984), p. 444.

[xv]Henry, op. cit. pp. 175-176.

[xvi]Max Lucado, *The Applause of Heaven* (Texas: Word Publishing, 1990), p. 12.

[xvii]Stephen C. Mott, *Biblical Ethics and Social Change* (New York: Oxford University Press, 1982), p. 23.

[xviii]Schaeffer, "A Christian View of Philosophy and Culture" 1:115.

[xix]Mott, op. cit. p. 27.

[xx]Dick Iverson, *Holiness: The Unique Escape from Oblivion* (New York: MFI Regionals, sp. 1992), p. 5-6.

[xxi]*Webster's* II New Riverside University Dictionary, op. cit. p. 1035.

[xxii]Henry, op. cit. pp. 350-353.

[xxiii]R. K. Harrison, ed., *Encyclopedia of Biblical and Christian Ethics* (Nashville, Tennessee: Thomas Nelson, Publishers, 1987), p. 226.

[xxiv]Walter C. Kaiser, *Toward Old Testament Ethics* (Michigan: Zondervan Publishing House, 1983), pp. 308-312.

[xxv]Harrison, op. cit. p. 229.

[xxvi] Douglas D. Webster, *Choices of the Heart* (Zondervan Publishing House, 1990), pp. 41-42.

[xxvii]James D. Cunningham and Anthony C. Fortosis, *Education in Christian Schools: A Perspective and Training Model* (Whittier, California: The Association of Christian Schools International, 1987), pp. 104-105.

[xxviii]Bonhoeffer, op. cit. p. 280.

[xxix]Schaeffer, *A Christian View of the Church* , p. 152.

[xxx]Kevin J. Conner, *The Church in the New Testament* (Oregon: Bible Temple Publishing, 1989), p. 78.

[xxxi]Dick Iverson, *Present Day Truths* (Oregon: Bible Temple Publishing, 1975), pp. 164-165.

[xxxii]Mott, op. cit. p. 133.

[xxxiii]Conner, p. 29.

[xxxiv]Schaeffer, *A Christian View of the Church*, op. cit. Vol. 4. p. 134.

[xxxv]D. Stuart Briscoe, *The Communicator's Commentary: Romans* (Texas: Word Books, Publisher, 1982), 6:142-143.

[xxxvi]Lucado, op. cit. p. 176.

[xxxvii]Briscoe, op. cit. p. 144.

[xxxviii]F. F. Bruce, *Tyndale New Testament Commentaries: Romans* (1985; rpt. Michigan: William B. Eerdmans Publishing Company, 1988), p. 138.

[xxxix]Lewis Sperry Chafer, *Major Bible Themes* (Michigan: Zondervan Publishing House, 1974), pp. 279-280.

[xl]Francis Foulkes, *Tyndale New Testament Commentaries: Ephesians* (Michigan: William B. Eerdmans Publishing Company, 1989), p. 166.

[xli]Colin Kruse, *Tyndale New Testament Commentaries: 2 Corinthians* (Michigan: William B. Eerdmans Publishing Company, 1989), p. 183.

[xlii]Ralph W. Harris, ed., *The Complete Bible Library; The New Testament Study Bible: Romans - Corinthians* (Missouri: The Complete Bible Library, 1989), 7:611.

[xliii]Schaeffer, *A Christian View of Spirituality,* 3:278-279.

[xliv]Webster, op. cit. pp. 102-103.

[xlv]Doug Sherman and William Hendricks, *Keeping Your Ethical Edge Sharp* (Colorado: Navepress, 1990), pp. 146-147.

[xlvi] Stanley Hauerwas and Wil Willimon, *Resident Aliens* (Nashville: Abingdon Press, 1989), p. 124

[xlvii] Richard J. Foster, *Money, Sex and Power: The Challenge of the Disciplined Life* (San Francisco: Harper & Row Publishers, 1985), pp.213-14.

[xlviii] Erwin W. Lutzer, *Pastor to Pastor: Tackling Problems of the Pulpit* (Chicago: Moody Press, 1987), 136.

[xlix] Cf. John Howard Yoder, "Revolutionary Subordination," in Politics of Jesus (Grand Rapids, MI: William B. Eerdmans Publishing Co., 1972), pp. 163ff.

[l] John 17:22-23.

[li] Acts 2:4.

[lii] Cf. Acts 4:32-37.

[liii] Jerome, "Letters 52," in *The Nicene and Post-Nicene Fathers*, 14 vols., Second Series, eds. Philip Schaff and Henry Wace (repr. Grand Rapids: Eerdmans, n.d.), 6: 94. (Hereafter cited as *The Nicene and Post-Nicene Fathers.*)

[liv] "A Biblical Style of Leadership?" *Leadership 2* (Fall, 1981): pp. 119-129.

[lv] John MacArthur, Jr., *Different by Design: Discovering God's Will for Today's Man and Woman* (Wheaton: Victor, 1994), p. 114.

[lvi] Richard N. Ostling, "The Second Reformation," *Time* (November 23, 1992). p. 54.

[lvii] For a more comprehensive study of this topic see refer to *Parenting to Impact Generations* by Dr. Donald I. Bernier

[lviii] Rankin, William W. *Confidentiality and Clergy: Churches, Ethics, and the Law.* Harrisburg, PA.: Morehouse Publishing Co., 1990, p. 78.

[lix] Shupe, Anson, ed. Wolves Within the Fold, Rutgers University Press, 1998, pp. 51-7.

[lx] "Clergy Salaries," Congregations, September/October, 2002

[lxi] "Study: Clergy salaries up but still not great for many," http://www.pulpitandpew.duke.edu/salary.html/ Viewed August 15, 2003.

153

[lxii] Neuhaus, Richard, Freedom for Ministry, Harper and Row, 1979, pp. 191-92.

[lxiii] Jeff Seat, et.al., "*The Prevalence and Contributing Factors of Sexual Misconduct among Southern Baptist Pastors in Six Southern States*" **The Journal of Pastoral Care**, Winter 1993, Vol. 47, No. 4.

[lxiv] John W. Thoburn and Jack O. Balswick, "*Demographic Data on Extra-Marital Sexual Behavior in the Ministry*" **Pastoral Psychology**, 1998, Vol. 46, No. 6; "*Rabbi's Odyssey Reflects Struggle on Sexual Abuse*" **The Washington Post,** February 2, 2003, p.A17.

[lxv] "*Broken Trust: A covenant of Clergy Sexual Ethics*," The Christian Life Commission of the Baptist General Convention of Texas.

[lxvi] Bill Flatt, "*The Misuse of Power and Sex in Helping Relationships*" **Restoration Quarterly**, January, 1993, Vol. 36, pp. 101-110; Pamela Cooper-White, "*Soul stealing: Power Relations in Pastoral Sexual Abuse*" **The Christian Century**, Feb. 20, 1991, pp. 196-99; Anson Shupe, ed., *Wolves within the Fold: Religious Leadership and Abuses of Power*, Piscataway, NJ: *Rutgers University Press*, 1998.

[lxvii] The entire issue of *Pastoral Pschology*, March, 1991, Vol. 39, No. 4 is dedicated to this problem.

[lxviii] Ragsdale, Katherine Hancock, *Boundary Wars: Intimacy and Distance in Healing Realtionships*, Plymouth, MI: Pilgrim Press, 1996.

[lxix] Seat, "*The Prevalence and Contributing Factors of Sexual Misconduct*"

Dr. Bernier's books include:

- *Shades of Gray: Discerning the Standard of Christian Ethics*
- *Powerful Living*
- *Fruitful Living*
- *Rise Up and Build: Transforming Principles in the Life and Ministry of Nehemiah.*
- *Principles & Practice of the Pastoral Ministry*
- *Christian Foundations*
- *Parenting to Impact Generations*

For more information contact:

Master Builder Ministries, Inc.
397 Bay Street
Fall River, Massachusetts 02724
(508) 730-1735
www.mbministries.org

or

Vision Publishing

1-800-9-VISION

www.visionpublishingservices.com

www.ingramcontent.com/pod-product-compliance
Lightning Source LLC
LaVergne TN
LVHW051125080426
835510LV00018B/2232